THE AMERICAN CONSTITUTION

PROBLEMS IN AMERICAN HISTORY

EDITOR

LOREN BARITZ

State University of New York, Albany

THE LEADERSHIP OF ABRAHAM LINCOLN
Don E. Fehrenbacher

THE AMERICAN CONSTITUTION
Paul Goodman

THE AMERICAN REVOLUTION
Richard J. Hooker

AMERICA IN THE COLD WAR
Walter LaFeber

ORIGINS OF THE COLD WAR, 1941–1947
Walter LaFeber

AMERICAN IMPERIALISM IN 1898
Richard H. Miller

TENSIONS IN AMERICAN PURITANISM
Richard Reinitz

THE GREAT AWAKENING
Darrett B. Rutman

WORLD WAR I AT HOME
David F. Trask

THE CRITICAL YEARS,
AMERICAN FOREIGN POLICY, 1793–1825
Patrick C. T. White

THE AMERICAN CONSTITUTION

EDITED BY

PAUL GOODMAN

University of California, Davis

JOHN WILEY & SONS, INC.

NEW YORK · LONDON · SYDNEY · TORONTO

Library of Congress Catalogue Card Number: 79-111356

Cloth: SBN 471 31370 X   Paper: SBN 471 31371 8

Printed in the United States of America

10 9 8 7 6 5 4 3 2 1

SERIES PREFACE

This series is an introduction to the most important problems in the writing and study of American history. Some of these problems have been the subject of debate and argument for a long time, although others only recently have been recognized as controversial. However, in every case, the student will find a vital topic, an understanding of which will deepen his knowledge of social change in America.

The scholars who introduce and edit the books in this series are teaching historians who have written history in the same general area as their individual books. Many of them are leading scholars in their fields, and all have done important work in the collective search for better historical understanding.

Because of the talent and the specialized knowledge of the individual editors, a rigid editorial format has not been imposed on them. For example, some of the editors believe that primary source material is necessary to their subjects. Some believe that their material should be arranged to show conflicting interpretations. Others have decided to use the selected materials as evidence for their own interpretations. The individual editors have been given the freedom to handle their books in the way that their own experience and knowledge indicate is best. The overall result is a series built up from the individual decisions of working scholars in the various fields, rather than one that conforms to a uniform editorial decision.

A common goal (rather than a shared technique) is the bridge of this series. There is always the desire to bring the reader as close to these problems as possible. One result of this objective is an emphasis on the nature and consequences of problems and events, with a de-emphasis of the more purely historiographical issues. The goal is to involve the student in the reality of crisis, the inevitability of ambiguity, and the excitement of finding a way through the historical maze.

Above all, this series is designed to show students how experienced historians read and reason. Although health is not contagious, intellectual engagement may be. If we show students something significant in a phrase or a passage that they otherwise may have missed, we will have accomplished part of our objective. When students see something that passed us by, then the process will have been made whole. This active and mutual involvement of editor and reader with a significant human problem will rescue the study of history from the smell and feel of dust.

Loren Baritz

CONTENTS

THE AMERICAN CONSTITUTION

INTRODUCTION

The United States is the oldest republic in the world. Established at a time when kings and aristocrats ruled almost everywhere, and popular rule was regarded as impractical, if not dangerous, America confounded those prophesying failure for this experiment in free government. The founding fathers were fully aware of the destructive forces, at home and abroad, that threatened the young nation. But they were also confident that by devising appropriate mechanisms of government they might escape the anarchy of weak government and the tyranny of strong government. The Federal Constitution was the result of a long, complex search for a framework of national authority that would secure individual liberty as well as communal order.

That search began when independence forced Americans to construct new constitutions for the United States and for the former colonies, now semi-sovereign states. Though the process of nation-building in the United States was unique, colored by the colonists' traditions and experiences, the Americans faced problems similar to those confronting the new nations established in Asia and Africa during the past twenty-five years.

For more than a decade following independence, Americans attempted to establish a nation that was strong yet free, that commanded support from its citizens and respect from other countries, that afforded people the chance to participate in decision making, and that inspired a common loyalty among the diverse elements scattered across a huge continent. Today other new nations struggle to hurdle the obstacles to nation-building that Americans overcame almost two hundred years ago. In the first set of selections below, a political scientist defines the crises of national development that were familiar to the founding fathers (revealed in brief excerpts from *The Federalist Papers*).

1

The Americans had few models to guide them and they fumbled at times as one might expect in any experiment. At first, they made as few changes as possible, creating a weak central government and leaving most of the power in the former colonies, now states. There had been much spontaneity in the resistance to England that often began in one colony and spread to another without prior planning. Because the colonists controlled some of the organs of government, such as the provincial legislatures, they could mount their attacks on British policy from centers of legitimate authority. And when the break with England came, anarchy did not ensue because local government remained largely in patriot hands and continued to function smoothly. Independence, therefore, strengthened the control of native elites who no longer had to operate under the restraints of British authority. The state governments, eventually sanctioned by newly drafted constitutions, levied taxes, raised armies, and maintained order. The process by which the revolutionaries reconstructed political authority is explored in the second set of selections. Even before the Declaration of Independence, Americans from different colonies had begun to work together in a common cause against Britain. Provincial legislatures sent delegates to the Stamp Act Congress in 1765 and to the Continental Congress (1774–1776) that coordinated the resistance and eventually voted for independence. Americans, however, feared central government—even their own—and they did not formally adopt a national constitution (The Articles of Confederation) until 1781 when the war was nearly over. Their fears stemmed from recent experiences with a parliament they regarded as tyrannical. Moreover, provincial elites who had acquired new power were reluctant to surrender it to a distant central government, even one that they created.

During the war, the Continental Congress established a national army, appointed a commander-in-chief in charge of both state and continental forces, conducted foreign affairs, and secured vital help from France; but Congress remained dependent on the states for funds and proved to be at the mercy of provincial parsimony and jealousies. Ratification of the Articles did little to change that. It left the states virtually sovereign and gave them the power to surrender only as much power to the national government as seemed absolutely necessary. Americans were deeply suspicious of power. Government, they thought, was a necessary evil because without it citizens could not enjoy order, security, or liberty. But government had a tendency to aggrandize power and become oppressive. The best defense against tyranny was to keep power close to the people where they could more effectively scrutinize public officials and zealously guard their freedom. This was the theory underlying the Articles of Confederation.

In less than a decade, Americans discovered this theory wanting. A loose confederation of sovereign states proved inadequate. The states were unwilling or unable to assume the responsibilities of a nation and the Confederation lacked the power to meet the needs of the Union. Merchants, artisans, and farmers failed to prosper and became caught in the grip of a postwar depression. At the same time, states raised taxes to pay off the revolutionary debt, making hard times even more difficult. Abroad, Americans encountered hostility that barred their goods from foreign markets. England refused to evacuate the West, according to the peace treaty, and Spain blocked free navigation of the Mississippi. The inability of the states or the nation to promote the common welfare aroused discontent. Massachusetts farmers rose in rebellion to save their farms from creditors and tax collectors; unpaid public security holders demanded that the states grant the Confederation the power to tax; merchants and artisans demanded protection from government against foreign competition.

Efforts to strengthen the Confederation by amending the Articles repeatedly floundered. Some people became alarmed. If citizens could not advance their interests under existing governments, they might abandon them as impractical and repudiate the republican experiment in favor of monarchy. By 1787 some believed that a new constitution for the nation was necessary.

Fortunately, the Americans quickly learned from experience and found in revolutionary political theory and procedures an escape from their dilemma. In 1787, for five months delegates from each state met in Philadelphia at a convention called by the Confederation to amend the Articles. Instead it drafted a new constitution. As the second group of selections suggest, the

Philadelphia Convention owed its success to the emergence in the preceding decades of a uniquely American conception of what a constitution is and how one is written.

The proposed new framework of government generated heated controversy. A majority of the states finally ratified the proposal, but only after prolonged debate. The sources of division in 1787 have in turn generated sharp conflict among historians who have tried to explain the origins of the Federal Constitution and the meaning of the struggle over ratification (subjects explored in the third and fourth set of selections).

One clue to understanding why some Americans favored and others opposed the new Constitution are the debates themselves. The next set of selection focuses on some of the major ideological differences between the contending forces. Finally, the last selection by Douglas Adair sheds fresh light on the founding fathers by reconstructing their sense of history and their deepest aspirations.

Despite its initial success, the Federal Constitution was no definitive solution to the problems of governing the nation. In 1861 the Union split apart, reunited only through a violent and bloody struggle. Today, as in the past, Americans face challenges that threaten their survival. Whether the instruments of government created by the revolutionary generation and developed during the last two centuries can secure order and justice at home and peace abroad in a world far more complex and dangerous than that of the founding fathers, remains unclear.

The agonizing process by which Americans created a nation out of thirteen colonies and attempted to reconcile their fear of power with their need for strong government and harmonize the individual's desire for liberty with the community's need for order is illuminated in the historical sources that follow.

PART ONE

America as a New Nation

The problems encountered by Americans in founding a nation in the late eighteenth century have also confronted other newly independent peoples. Since 1945, dozens of new nations, rising from the ruins of colonial empires, have sought to satisfy the demands of people throughout the world for self-determination and a better life. The experiences of countries such as India, Nigeria, the Congo, and Vietnam, to mention a few, have disappointed expectations. Foreign rule has given way to new regimes that lack stability and even the ability to survive. Though the Americans were notably successful in transforming colonies into a powerful nation, the founding fathers were deeply aware of the dangers they faced, as the selection below from *The Federalist Papers* indicates. Written by Alexander Hamilton, James Madison, and John Jay, *The Federalist Papers* were designed to win support for a new Federal Constitution in 1787–1788. The problems confronting the Americans then, to which the framers of the Constitution addressed themselves, can be understood more clearly by identifying the crises of political development that new nations experience. The precise form the crises took in the United States was unique, shaped by distinctive traditions, social arrangements, and cultural patterns that had developed before independence. In the second selection, Lucian Pye, a political scientist, analyzes the process of nation-building. Pye notes that nations undergo a crisis of participation to determine who will rule. Unlike most of the new nations of Asia and Africa whose citizens were excluded from political participation before

5

independence, the American colonists had a strong tradition of local self-government and a majority of the adult white males could vote even though there were property qualifications. But they had no direct experience in central government since that responsibility had been the exclusive prerogative of the Crown and Parliament. Creating a national political arena in which citizens could effectively participate in the governing of the nation proved vexing. The states surrendered only minimal authority to the first central government under the Articles of Confederation, which could neither tax nor act directly upon citizens. Similarly, the task of integrating diverse elements into a viable nation proved equally troublesome. Rivalries and jealousies among the states had resulted in the establishment of a weak Confederation and even the new Constitution inaugurated in 1789 carefully divided power between the states and the nation. Though Americans had the advantages of common cultural and religious traditions over other new countries that lack even a common language, the crisis of national political integration was prolonged and not resolved until the Civil War clearly made the states subordinate to the Union.

By analyzing how Americans confronted the crisis of political development specified by Pye, and by comparing their experiences with those of other countries, we can gain a clearer understanding of how modern nations develop and of the distinctive features of the American case.

THE FOUNDING FATHERS
AS NATION-BUILDERS

1 FROM *Alexander Hamilton*
The Federalist Papers, No. 1

After an unequivocal experience of the inefficiency of the subsisting Federal government, you are called upon to deliberate on a new Constitution for the United States of America. The subject speaks its own importance; comprehending in its consequences nothing less than the existence of the UNION, the safety and welfare of the parts of which it is composed, the fate of an empire in many respects the most interesting in the world. It has been frequently remarked that it seems to have been reserved to the people of this country, by their conduct and example, to decide the important question, whether societies of men are really capable or not of establishing good government from reflection and choice, or whether they are forever destined to depend for their political constitutions on accident and force. If there be any truth in the remark, the crisis at which we are arrived may with propriety be regarded as the era in which that decision is to be made; and a wrong election of the part we shall act may, in this view, deserve to be considered as the general misfortune of mankind. . . .

It may perhaps be thought superfluous to offer arguments to

SOURCE: Alexander Hamilton in *The Federalist Papers*, No. 1, pp. 3, 7 (New York: Random House, Inc., Modern Library Edition, 1941).

prove the utility of the UNION, a point, no doubt, deeply engraved on the hearts of the great body of the people in every State, and one, which it may be imagined, has no adversaries. But the fact is, that we already hear it whispered in the private circles of those who oppose the new Constitution, that the thirteen States are of too great extent for any general system, and that we must of necessity resort to separate confederacies of distinct portions of the whole. This doctrine will, in all probability, be gradually propagated, till it has votaries enough to countenance an open avowal of it. For nothing can be more evident, to those who are able to take an enlarged view of the subject, than the alternative of an adoption of the new Constitution or a dismemberment of the Union. . . .

2 FROM *Alexander Hamilton*
The Federalist Papers, No. 4

As the safety of the whole is the interest of the whole, and cannot be provided for without government, either one or more or many, let us inquire whether one good government is not, relative to the object in question, more competent than any other given number whatever.

One government can collect and avail itself of the talents and experience of the ablest men, in whatever part of the Union they may be found. It can move on uniform principles of policy. It can harmonize, assimilate, and protect the several parts and members, and extend the benefit of its foresight and precautions to each. In the formation of treaties, it will regard the interest of the whole, and the particular interests of the parts as connected with that of the whole. It can apply the resources and power of the whole to the defence of any particular part, and that more easily and expeditiously than State governments or separate confederacies can possibly do, for want of concert and unity of

SOURCE: Alexander Hamilton in *The Federalist Papers*, No. 4, pp. 19–22 (New York: Random House, Inc., Modern Library Edition, 1944).

system. It can place the militia under one plan of discipline, and, by putting their officers in a proper line of subordination to the Chief Magistrate, will, as it were, consolidate them into one corps, and thereby render them more efficient than if divided into thirteen or into three or four distinct independent companies. . . .

But whatever may be our situation, whether firmly united under one national government, or split into a number of confederacies, certain it is, that foreign nations will know and view it exactly as it is; and they will act towards us accordingly. If they see that our national government is efficient and well administered, our trade prudently regulated, our militia properly organized and disciplined, our resources and finances discreetly managed, our credit re-established, our people free, contented, and united, they will be much more disposed to cultivate our friendship than provoke our resentment. If, on the other hand, they find us either destitute of an effectual government (each State doing right or wrong, as to its rulers may seem convenient), or split into three or four independent and probably discordant republics or confederacies, one inclining to Britain, another to France, and a third to Spain, and perhaps played off against each other by the three, what a poor, pitiful figure will America make in their eyes! How liable would she become not only to their contempt, but to their outrage; and how soon would dear-bought experience proclaim that when a people or family so divide, it never fails to be against themselves.

THE CRISES IN
POLITICAL DEVELOPMENT

3 FROM   *Lucian W. Pye*
        Aspects of Political Development

For purposes of political analysis it is . . . necessary to . . . ask what must happen within the political system when a society experiences the stress . . . identified with the political modernization syndrome. What happens to a society when there is a broad demand for equality and participation, when there is a need for increased capacity or governmental capabilities, and when the processes of differentiation and specialization tend to become more acute?

Some members of the Committee on Comparative Politics of the Social Science Research Council have suggested that it may be useful to conceptualize the processes of political development as involving essentially six crises that may be met in different sequences but all of which must be successfully dealt with for a society to become a modern nation-state.

THE IDENTITY CRISIS

The first and most fundamental crisis is that of achieving a common sense of identity. The people in a new state must come

SOURCE: Lucian W. Pye, *Aspects of Political Development*, pp. 62–67 (Boston: Little, Brown and Co., 1966). Reprinted by permission of the publisher.

to recognize their national territory as being their true homeland, and they must feel as individuals that their own personal identities are in part defined by their identification with their territorially delimited country. In most of the new states traditional forms of identity ranging from tribe or caste to ethnic and linguistic groups compete with the sense of larger national identity.

The identity crisis also involves the resolution of the problem of traditional heritage and modern practices, the dilemma of parochial sentiments and cosmopolitan practices, which we have emphasized. As long as people feel pulled between two worlds and without roots in any society they cannot have the firm sense of identity necessary for building a stable, modern nation-state.

THE LEGITIMACY CRISIS

Closely related to the identity crisis is the problem of achieving agreement about the legitimate nature of authority and the proper responsibilities of government. In many new states the crisis of legitimacy is a straightforward constitutional problem: What should be the relationship between central and local authorities? What are the proper limits of the bureaucracy, or of the army, in the nation's political life? Or possibly the conflict is over how much of the colonial structure of government should be preserved in an independent state.

In other new states the question of legitimacy is more diffuse, and it involves sentiments about what should be the underlying spirit of government and the primary goals of national effort. For example, in some Moslem lands there is a deep desire that the state should in some fashion reflect the spirit of Islam. In other societies the issue of legitimacy involves questions about how far the governmental authorities should directly push economic development as compared with other possible goals. Above all, in transitional societies there can be a deep crisis of authority because all attempts at ruling are challenged by different people for different reasons, and no leaders are able to gain a full command of legitimate authority.

THE PENETRATION CRISIS

The critical problems of administration in the new states give rise to the penetration crisis, which involves the problems of government in reaching down into the society and effecting basic policies. As we have noted, in traditional societies government had limited demands to make on the society, and in most transitional systems the governments are far more ambitious. This is particularly true if the rulers seek to accelerate the pace of economic development and social change. To carry out significant development policies a government must be able to reach down to the village level and touch the daily lives of people.

Yet, as we have observed, a dominant characteristic of transitional societies is the gap between the world of the ruling elite and that of the masses of the people who are still oriented toward their parochial ways. The penetration problem is that of building up the effectiveness of the formal institutions by government and of establishing confidence and rapport between rulers and subjects. Initially governments often find it difficult to motivate the population or to change its values and habits in order to bring support to programs of national development. On the other hand, at times the effectiveness of the government in breaking down old patterns of control can unleash widespread demands for a greater influence on governmental policies. When this occurs the result is another crisis, that of participation.

THE PARTICIPATION CRISIS

As we noted in seeking to define political development, one dimension of the concept involves an expansion of popular participation. The participation crisis occurs when there is uncertainty over the appropriate rate of expansion and when the influx of new participants creates serious strains on the existing institutions. As new segments of the population are brought into the political process, new interests and new issues begin to arise so that the continuity of the old polity is broken and there is the need to reestablish the entire structure of political relations.

In a sense the participation crisis arises out of the emergence of interest groups and the formation of a party system. The question in many new states is whether the expansion in participation is likely to be effectively organized into specific interest groups or whether the pressures will lead only to mass demands and widespread feelings of anomie. It should also be noted that the appearance of a participation crisis does not necessarily signal pressures for democratic processes. The participation crisis can be organized as in totalitarian states to provide the basis for manipulated mass organizations and demonstrational politics.

INTEGRATION CRISIS

This crisis covers the problems of relating popular politics to governmental performance, and thus it represents the effective and compatible solution of both the penetration and the participation crises. The problem of integration therefore deals with the extent to which the entire polity is organized as a system of interacting relationships, first among the offices and agencies of government, and then among the various groups and interests seeking to make demands upon the system, and finally in the relationships between officials and articulating citizens.

In many of the transitional systems there may be many different groupings of interests, but they hardly interact with each other, and at best each seeks to make its separate demands upon the government. The government must seek to cope with all these demands simultaneously. Yet at the same time the government itself may not be well integrated. The result is a low level of general performance throughout the political system.

THE DISTRIBUTION CRISIS

The final crisis in the development process involves questions about how governmental powers are to be used to influence the distribution of goods, services, and values throughout the society. Who is to benefit from government, and what should the government be doing to bring greater benefits to different segments of the society?

Much of the stress on economic development and the popularity of socialist slogans in the new states is a reflection of the basic crisis. In some cases governments seek to meet the problem by directly intervening in the distribution of wealth; in other cases the approach is to strengthen the opportunities and potentialities of the disadvantaged groups.

THE SEQUENCES OF DEVELOPMENT

The particular pattern of development in any country depends largely upon the sequence in which these crises arise and the ways in which they are resolved. It is noteworthy that in the history of England, the model of modern democracies, development tended to follow a path in which the crises arose somewhat separately and largely according to the order in which we have just outlined them. The English developed a sense of national identity early, the issue of the legitimacy of the monarchy and government was well established before the problem of expanding participation appeared and, finally, serious issues of distribution did not arise until after the political system was relatively well integrated.

In contrast, development of the continental European system followed more chaotic patterns. In Italy and Germany the prelude of nation-building did not involve a resolution of the issue of national identity. In France questions of legitimacy and the realities of inadequate integration have persistently frustrated national performance and intensified the crisis of distribution. It was, indeed, the cumulativeness and simultaneity of the crises on the continent that produced the striking differences between the European and the British systems.

The story in modern Asia and Africa seems to be closer to the continental experience than either the British or American. In most of the new states the crises are all appearing simultaneously, and governments are, for example, striving to use the distribution crisis to resolve the identity problem. The efforts to raise the standards of living in these cases are in large part related to creating feelings of basic loyalty to the nation, and this procedure raises the question of how stable such states can become if their citizens' sense of identity is tied too closely to the effectiveness of particular policies.

... Ultimately any useful theory of political development must come to grips with the types of problems we have subsumed under this list of crises.

PART TWO

Nation-Building, American Style

Written constitutions framed by specially chosen conventions became a vital part of the process of nation-building in the United States. At the time of American independence there were no accepted procedures for establishing a new regime. The American was the first anticolonial revolution and the United States the first new nation in modern times. The Americans proceeded by trial and error but their direction was deeply influenced by political thought generated in the struggle with Britain.

At the heart of the controversy between the colonists and the mother country were different conceptions of the British Constitution. Opposed to newly enacted British taxes and controls, the Americans sought to establish limits on the power of Parliament. They insisted that the British Constitution barred Parliament from taxing the colonists without their consent. The English replied that the Constitution lodged sovereign power in the Crown and Parliament. Denied protection of the Constitution, the Americans ultimately appealed to the laws of nature that they claimed guaranteed for each man life, liberty, and property as inalienable rights. But the British replied that the Constitution protected natural rights and came as close as man-made law could to embody the laws of nature. By 1776 the only alternative left to the Americans was submission or independence. Arguing that power ultimately derived from the people, and that they were not represented in Parliament, the colonists denied the legitimacy of British rule and set up governments of their own choice.

Independence thus brought Americans face to face with the task of establishing new regimes and defining their constitutional basis. In the process, they worked out a new conception of a constitution as well as ingenious procedures for devising new frameworks of government. Traditionally, a constitution simply meant the political arrangements prevailing at a given time that changed as new needs arose. The British Constitution thus comprised all the laws and customs of the realm, and as new ones evolved, they became an integral part of the constitution. Since Parliament traditionally had the power to tax, and the colonies were subordinate to the Crown and Parliament, the British could not accept the American view that the Americans were exempt from British taxation. The Americans did not deliberately formulate new principles. They thought that "no taxation without representation" was settled British doctrine. Yet out of necessity they were led to transform the definition of a constitution. As Bernard Bailyn shows in the first section below, the colonists argued that a constitution embodies *fundamental* or *natural* law that limits the power of government. Legislative bodies enact *statutory* law, which can be altered from time to time, but must conform to the requirements of natural law (which does not alter and which protects individuals from arbitrary power, such as being taxed without their consent). In other words, constitutions lay down the rules of the game by which men agree to govern themselves; they fix the powers of judges, legislators, and executives; constitutions check and limit authority, secure civil liberties, and thereby become guarantors of freedom.

This notion of a constitution as a fixed source of authority that imposes limits upon the exercise of power, guided Americans after independence. They conceived of constitutions as the authentic expression of the people, the indispensable basis of popular government—its source of legitimacy. In the second selection, Robert R. Palmer shows that the Americans did more than proclaim democratic ideals; they invented the Constitutional Convention as a practical means of framing fundamental law and inaugurating new regimes based on popular consent. The Constitutional Convention was not obvious to the revolutionary generation. At first, acting without precedent and not fully aware of the implications of their new conception of a constitution, Americans let provisional revolutionary legislatures write state constitutions. But it was eventually concluded that legislatures were not appropriate bodies since if they could make a constitution, they could also change it at will. Thus the logic of the new definition of a constitution led people to realize that a specially chosen, independent body, preferably one freshly picked by the people, was necessary.

In 1787 when Americans wished to amend the Articles of Confederation, they called a convention. By that time, the conception of a constitution as fundamental law framed by a specially chosen convention had flowered from the revolutionary notion of the people as the source of power into practical principles and procedures of free government. The American example had far-reaching influence. The French Revolution was the start of a century of revolution in Europe that replaced autocratic governments with popular regimes partly based on theories and practices first worked out by the United States.

THE CONCEPT
OF A CONSTITUTION

4 FROM   *Bernard Bailyn*
The Ideological Origins of the American Revolution

. . . The colonists' attitude to the whole world of politics and government was fundamentally shaped by the root assumption that they, as Britishers, shared in a unique inheritance of liberty. The English people, they believed, though often threatened by despots who had risen in their midst, had managed to maintain, to a greater degree and for a longer period of time than any other people, a tradition of the successful control of power and of those evil tendencies of human nature that would prevent its proper uses.

In view of the natural obstacles that stood in the way of such a success and in view of the dismal history of other nations, this, as the colonists saw it, had been an extraordinary achievement. But it was not a miraculous one. It could be explained historically. The ordinary people of England, they believed, were descended from simple, sturdy Saxons who had known liberty in the very childhood of the race and who, through the centuries, had retained the desire to preserve it. But it had taken more than desire. Reinforcing, structuring, expressing the liberty-loving

SOURCE: Bernard Bailyn, *The Ideological Origins of the American Revolution*, pp. 66–69, 175–176, 181–184 (Cambridge: The Belknap Press of Harvard University Press, 1967). Reprinted by permission of the publisher and the author.

temper of the people, there was England's peculiar "constitution," described by John Adams, in words almost every American agreed with before 1763, as "the most perfect combination of human powers in society which finite wisdom has yet contrived and reduced to practice for the preservation of liberty and the production of happiness."

The word "constitution" and the concept behind it was of central importance to the colonists' political thought; their entire understanding of the crisis in Anglo-American relations rested upon it. So strategically located was this idea in the minds of both English and Americans, and so great was the pressure placed upon it in the course of a decade of pounding debate that in the end it was forced apart, along the seam of a basic ambiguity, to form the two contrasting concepts of constitutionalism that have remained characteristic of England and America ever since.

At the start of the controversy, however, the most distinguishing feature of the colonists' view of the constitution was its apparent traditionalism. Like their contemporaries in England and like their predecessors for centuries before, the colonists at the beginning of the Revolutionary controversy understood by the word "constitution" not, as we would have it, a written document or even an unwritten but deliberately contrived design of government and a specification of rights beyond the power of ordinary legislation to alter; they thought of it, rather, as the constituted—that is, existing—arrangement of governmental institutions, laws, and customs together with the principles and goals that animated them. So John Adams wrote that a political constitution is like "the constitution of the human body"; "certain contextures of the nerves, fibres, and muscles, or certain qualities of the blood and juices" some of which "may properly be called *stamina vitae,* or essentials and fundamentals of the constitution; parts without which life itself cannot be preserved a moment." A constitution of government, analogously, Adams wrote, is "a frame, a scheme, a system, a combination of powers for a certain end, namely,—the good of the whole community."

The elements of this definition were traditional, but it was nevertheless distinctive in its emphasis on the animating principles, the *stamina vitae,* those "fundamental laws and rules of the constitution, which ought never to be infringed." Belief that a proper system of laws and institutions should be suffused with, should express, essences and fundamentals—moral rights, reason, justice—had never been absent from English notions of the constitution. But not since the Levellers had protested against Parliament's supremacy in the mid-seventeenth century had these considerations seemed so important as they did to the Americans of the mid-eighteenth century. Nor could they ever have appeared more distinct in their content. For if the ostensible purpose of all government was the good of the people, the particular goal of the English constitution—"its end, its use, its designation, drift, and scope"—was known to all, and declared by all, to be the attainment of liberty. This was its peculiar "grandeur" and excellence; it was for this that it should be prized "next to our Bibles, above the privileges of this world." It was for this that it should be blessed, supported and maintained, and transmitted "in full, to posterity." . . .

Certain of the Tories understood also with special clarity the meaning of changes that were taking place in other areas of thought. They grasped, and exclaimed against in protest, the transformation of the notion of what a constitution was and of the nature of the rights that constitutions existed to protect. "What is the constitution," Charles Inglis demanded in his anguished reply to *Common Sense*—what is "that word so often used—so little understood—so much perverted? It is, as I conceive—*that assemblage of laws, customs, and institutions which form the general system according to which the several powers of the state are distributed and their respective rights are secured to the different members of the community.*" It was still for him, as it had been traditionally, what John Adams had described a decade earlier as "a frame, a scheme, a system, a combination of powers": the existing arrangement of governmental institutions, laws, and customs together with the animating principles, the *stamina vitae,* that gave them purpose and direction. But so far toward a different conception of constitutionalism had American thought shifted after 1765 that by 1776 Inglis' quite traditional definition could only be uttered as the *cri de coeur* of one bypassed by history.

The first suggestions of change came early in the period, the full conclusion only at the very end. At the start what would emerge as the central feature of American constitutionalism was only an emphasis and a peculiarity of tone within an otherwise familiar discourse. While some writers, like Richard Bland, continued to refer to "a legal constitution, that is, a legislature," and others spoke of "the English constitution . . . a nice piece of machinery which has undergone many changes and alterations," most of the writers saw the necessity of emphasizing principles above institutions, and began to grasp the consequences of doing so. . . .

. . . The transition to more advanced ground was forced forward by the continuing need, after 1764, to distinguish fundamentals from institutions and from the actions of government so that they might serve as limits and controls. Once its utility was perceived and demonstrated, this process of disengaging principles from institutions and from the positive actions of government and then of conceiving of them as fixed sets of rules and boundaries, went on swiftly.

In 1768 Samuel Adams, accustomed to drawing more extreme conclusions than most of his contemporaries, wrote in a series of letters in behalf of the Massachusetts House of Representatives that "the constitution is fixed; it is from thence that the supreme legislative as well as the supreme executive derives its authority," and he incorporated the same language into the famous Massachusetts Circular Letter of that year. At the same time a Philadelphian, William Hicks, wrote that if one were to concede that statutes were "a part of [the] constitution" simply because they were once promulgated by government, one would have no basis for restraining the actions of any government. There is nothing sacrosanct, he wrote, in the "variant, inconsistent form of government which we have received at different periods of time"; they were accidental in origins, and their defects should be corrected by comparison with ideal models. In 1769 the emerging logic was carried further by Zubly, who flatly distinguished legislatures from the constitution, and declared that the existing Parliament "derives its authority and power from the constitution, and not the constitution from Parliament." The constitution, he wrote, "is permanent and ever the same," and Parliament "can no more make laws which are against the constitution or the unalterable privileges of British subjects than it can alter the constitution itself . . . The power of Parliament, and of every branch of it, has its bounds assigned by the constitution."

In 1770 the constitution was said to be "a line which marks out the enclosure;" in 1773 it was "the standing measure of the proceedings of government" of which rulers are "by no means to attempt an alteration . . . without public consent"; in 1774 it was a "model of government"; in 1775 it was "certain great first principles" on whose "certainty and permanency . . . the rights of both the ruler and the subjects depend; nor may they be altered or changed by ruler or people, but [only] by the whole collective body . . . nor may they be touched by the legislator." Finally, in 1776 there came conclusive pronouncements. Two pamphlets of that year, brilliant sparks thrown off by the clash of Revolutionary politics in Pennsylvania, lit up the final steps of the path that led directly to the first constitutions of the American states. "A constitution and a form of government," the author of *Four Letters on Important Subjects* wrote, "are frequently confounded together and spoken of as synonymous things, whereas they are not only different but are established for different purposes." All nations have governments, "but few, or perhaps none, have truly a constitution." The primary function of a constitution was to mark out the boundaries of governmental powers—hence in England, where there was no constitution, there were no limits (save for the effect of trial by jury) to what the legislature might do. In order to confine the ordinary actions of government, the constitution must be grounded in some fundamental source of authority, some "higher authority than the giving out temporary laws." This special authority could be gained if the constitution were created by "an act of *all*," and it would acquire permanence if it were embodied "in some written charter." Defects, of course, might be discovered and would have to be repaired: there would have to be some procedure by which to alter the constitution without disturbing its controlling power as fundamental law. For this, the means "are easy":

"some article in the constitution may provide that at the expiration of every seven or any other number of years a *provincial jury* shall be elected to inquire if any inroads have been made in the constitution, and to have power to remove them; but not to make alterations, unless a clear majority of all the inhabitants shall so direct."

Thus created and thus secured, the constitution could effectively designate what "part of their liberty" the people are to sacrifice to the necessity of having government, by furnishing answers to "the two following questions: first, what shall the form of government be? And secondly, what shall be its power?" In addition, "it is the part of a constitution to fix the manner in which the officers of government shall be chosen, and determine the principal outlines of their power, their time of duration, manner of commissioning them, etc." Finally, "all the great rights which man never mean, nor ever ought, to lose should be *guaranteed*, not *granted*, by the constitution, for at the forming a constitution, we ought to have in mind that whatever is left to be secured by law only may be altered by another law."

The same ideas, in some ways even more clearly worked out, appear in the second Pennsylvania pamphlet of 1776, *The Genuine Principles of the Ancient Saxon or English Constitution*, which was largely composed of excerpts from Obadiah Hulme's *An Historical Essay on the English Constitution*, published in London in 1771, a book both determinative and representative of the historical understanding that lay behind the emerging American constitutionalism. Here too was stated the idea of a constitution as a *"set of fundamental rules* by which even the supreme power of the state shall be governed" and which the legislature is absolutely forbidden to alter. But in this pamphlet there are more explicit explanations of how such documents come into being and of their permanence and importance. They are to be formed "by a convention of the delegates of the people appointed for that express purpose," the pamphlet states, and they are never to be "added to, diminished from, nor altered in any respect by any power besides the power which first framed [them]." They are to remain permanent, and so to have the most profound effect on the lives of people. "Men entrusted with the formation of civil constitutions should remember they are *painting for eternity*: that the smallest defect or redundancy in the system they frame may prove the destruction of millions."

THE PEOPLE AS
CONSTITUENT POWER

5 FROM   *Robert R. Palmer*
The Age of the Democratic Revolution: The Struggle

If it be asked what the American Revolution distinctively contributed to the world's stock of ideas, the answer might go somewhat along these lines. It did not contribute primarily a social
doctrine—for although a certain skepticism toward social rank was
an old American attitude, and possibly even a gift to mankind, it
long antedated the Revolution, which did not so much cut down,
as prevent the growth of, an aristocracy of European type. It did
not especially contribute economic ideas—for the Revolution had
nothing to teach on the production or distribution of goods, and
the most advanced parties objected to private wealth only when
it became too closely associated with government. They aimed at
a separation of economic and political spheres, by which men of
wealth, while free to get rich, should not have a disproportionate
influence on government, and, on the other hand, government
and public emoluments should not be used as a means of livelihood for an otherwise impecunious and unproductive upper class.

The American Revolution was a political movement, concerned
with liberty, and with power. Most of the ideas involved were by
no means distinctively American. There was nothing peculiarly

SOURCE: R. R. Palmer, *The Age of the Democratic Revolution*, pp. 213–
217, 228–229 (Princeton University Press and the Oxford University Press,
1964). Reprinted by permission of the publishers.

American in the concepts, purely as concepts, of natural liberty and equality. They were admitted by conservatives, and were taught in the theological faculty at the Sorbonne. Nor could American claim any exclusive understanding of the ideas of government by contract or consent, or the sovereignty of the people, of political representation, or the desirability of independence from foreign rule, or natural rights, or the difference between natural law and positive law, or between certain fundamental laws and ordinary legislation, or the separation of powers, or the federal union of separate states. All these ideas were perfectly familiar in Europe, and that is why the American Revolution was of such interest to Europeans.

THE DISTINCTIVENESS OF AMERICAN POLITICAL IDEAS

The most distinctive work of the Revolution was in finding a method, and furnishing a model, for putting these ideas into practical effect. It was in the implementation of similar ideas that Americans were more successful than Europeans. "In the last fifty years," wrote General Bonaparte to Citizen Talleyrand in 1797, "there is only one thing that I can see that we have really defined, and that is the sovereignty of the people. But we have had no more success in determining what is constitutional, than in allocating the different powers of government." And he said more peremptorily, on becoming Emperor in 1804, that the time had come "to constitute the Nation." He added: "I am the constituent power."

The problem throughout much of America and Europe, for half a century, was to "constitute" new government, and in a measure new societies. The problem was to find a constituent power. Napoleon offered himself to Europe in this guise. The Americans solved the problem by the device of the constitutional convention, which, revolutionary in origin, soon became institutionalized in the public law of the United States.

The constitutional convention in theory embodied the sovereignty of the people. The people chose it for a specific purpose, not to govern, but to set up institutions of government. The convention, acting as the sovereign people, proceeded to draft a constitution and a declaration of rights. Certain "natural" or "in-alienable" rights of the citizen were thus laid down at the same time as the powers of government. It was the constitution that created the powers of government, defined their scope, gave them legality, and balanced them one against another. The constitution was written and comprised in a single document. The constitution and accompanying declaration, drafted by the convention, must, in the developed theory, be ratified by the people. The convention thereupon disbanded and disappeared, lest its members have a vested interest in the offices they created. The constituent power went into abeyance, leaving the work of government to the authorities now constituted. The people, having exercised sovereignty, now came under government. Having made law, they came under law. They put themselves voluntarily under restraint. At the same time, they put restraint upon government. All government was limited government; all public authority must keep within the bounds of the constitution and of the declared rights. There were two levels of law, a higher law or constitution that only the people could make or amend, through constitutional conventions or bodies similarly empowered; and a statutory law, to be made and unmade, within the assigned limits, by legislators to whom the constitution gave this function.

Such was the theory, and it was a distinctively American one. European thinkers, in all their discussion of a political or social contract, of government by consent and of sovereignty of the people, had not clearly imagined the people as actually contriving a constitution and creating the organs of government. They lacked the idea of the people as a constituent power. Even in the French Revolution the idea developed slowly; members of the French National Assembly, long after the Tennis Court oath, continued to feel that the constitution which they were writing, to be valid, had to be accepted by the King as a kind of equal with whom the nation had to negotiate. Nor, indeed, would the King tolerate any other view. On the other hand, we have seen how at Geneva in 1767 the democrats advanced an extreme version of citizen sovereignty, holding that the people created the constitution and the public offices by an act of will; but they failed to get beyond a simple direct democracy; they had no idea of two levels of law, or of limited government, or of a delegated and representative legislative authority, or of a sovereign people which, after acting as a god from the machine in a constituent convention, retired to the more modest status of an electorate, and let its theoretical sovereignty become inactive.

The difficulty with the theory was that the conditions under which it could work were seldom present. No people really starts *de novo;* some political institutions always already exist; there is never a *tabula rasa,* or state of nature, or Chart Blanche as Galloway posited for conservative purposes. Also, it is difficult for a convention engaged in writing a constiution not to be embroiled in daily politics and problems of government. And it is hard to live voluntarily under restraint. In complex societies, or in times of crisis, either government or people or some part of the people may feel obliged to go beyond the limits that a constitution has laid down.

In reality, the idea of the people as a constituent power, with its corollaries, developed unclearly, gradually, and sporadically during the American Revolution. It was adumbrated in the Declaration of Independence: the people may "institute new government." Jefferson, among the leaders, perhaps conceived the idea most clearly. It is of especial interest, however, to see how the "people" themselves, that is, certain lesser and unknown or poorer or unsatisfied persons, contributed to these distinctive American ideas by their opposition to the Revolutionary elite.

There were naturally many Americans who felt that no change was needed except expulsion of the British. With the disappearance of the British governors, and collapse of the old governor's councils, the kind of men who had been active in the colonial assemblies, and who now sat as provincial congresses or other *de facto* revolutionary bodies, were easily inclined to think that they should keep the management of affairs in their own hands. Some parallel can be seen with what happened in Europe. There was a revolution, or protest, of constituted bodies against authorities set above them, and a more popular form of revolution, or protest, which aimed at changing the character or membership of these constituted bodies themselves. As at Geneva the General Council rebelled against the patriciate, without wishing to admit new citizens to the General Council; as in Britain the Whigs asserted the powers of Parliament against the King, without wishing to change the composition of Parliament; as in Belgium, in 1789, the Estates party declared independence from the Emperor, while maintaining the preexisting estates; as in France, also in 1789, the nobility insisted that the King govern through the Estates-General, but objected to the transformation of the three estates into a new kind of national body; as in the Dutch provinces in 1795 the Estates-General, after expelling the Prince of Orange, tried to remain itself unchanged, and resisted the election of a "convention"; so, in America in 1776, the assemblies that drove out the officers of the King, and governed their respective states under revolutionary conditions, sought to keep control of affairs in their own hands, and to avoid reconstitution at the hands of the "people."

Ten states gave themselves new constitutions in 1776 and 1777. In nine of these states, however, it was the ordinary assembly, that is, the revolutionary government of the day, that drafted and proclaimed the constitution. In the tenth, Pennsylvania, a constituent convention met, but it soon had to take on the burden of daily government in addition. In Connecticut and Rhode Island the colonial charters remained in force, and the authorities constituted in colonial times (when governors and councils had already been elected) remained unchanged in principle for half a century. In Massachusetts the colonial charter remained in effect until 1780.

Thus in no state, when independence was declared, did a true constituent convention meet, and, as it were, calmly and rationally devise government out of a state of nature. There was already, however, some recognition of the principle that constitutions cannot be made merely by governments, that a more fundamental power is needed to produce a constitution than to pass ordinary laws or carry on ordinary executive duties. Thus, in New Hampshire, New York, Delaware, Maryland, North Carolina, and Georgia, the assemblies drew up constitutions only after soliciting authority for that purpose from the voters. In Maryland and North Carolina there was a measure of popular ratification. . . .

The idea that sovereignty lay with the people, and not with states or their governments, made possible in America a new kind of federal structure unknown in Europe. The Dutch and Swiss federations were unions of component parts, close permanent alliances between disparate corporate members. For them no other structure was possible, because there was as yet no Dutch or Swiss people except in a cultural sense. It was in the Dutch revolution of 1795 and the Swiss revolution of 1798 that these two bundles of provinces or cantons were first proclaimed as political nations. In America it was easier to make the transition from a league of states, set up during the Revolution, to a more integral union set up in the United States constitution of 1787. The new idea was that, instead of the central government drawing its powers from the states, both central and state governments should draw their powers from the same source; the question was the limit between these two sets of derived powers. The citizen, contrariwise, was simultaneously a citizen both of the United States and of his own state. He was the sovereign, not they. He chose to live under two constitutions, two sets of laws, two sets of courts and officials; theoretically, he had created them all, reserving to himself, under each set, certain liberties specified in declarations of rights.

PART THREE

Origins of the Federal Constitution

Writing and revising constitutions consumed the energies of the leading men in the revolutinary generation. In less than fifteen years after independence, Americans had written more than a dozen constitutions for the states and two for the nation. The quest for an appropriate framework for the national government began in 1776 with the drafting of the Articles of Confederation that was finally ratified in 1781 and loosely joined the states together but left them virtually sovereign. Fear of central government, rooted in their experiences as colonists and in the struggle with Parliament, as well as fear of one another, made Americans unwilling to vest substantial authority in a government distant from local scrutiny and control.

Yet almost from the outset the Articles proved defective. The Confederation lacked the power to raise money, or to fund the revolutionary debt; it failed to gain access for American products in foreign markets and it was powerless to protect vital national interests that conflicted with those of Spain and England. The economic recession in the mid-1780s and the outbreak of Shays' rebellion in Massachusetts among discontented farmers aroused apprehension that the Union might disintegrate. No individual was more alarmed than James Madison who had gained firsthand knowledge of the Confederation's weaknesses as a delegate to Congress from Virginia. Like most Americans, Madison believed that a strong central government was potentially dangerous but he thought that an ineffective central government was more dangerous. Rivalries between the states and conflict within the various commonwealths might degenerate into tyranny if people concluded that only a strong man or a king could establish order and restore prosperity. In the following selection, Madison analyzes the defects of the Confederation and advocates a new constitution that would avoid the twin dangers of anarchy and tyranny.

Not everyone shared Madison's gloomy opinion of the Confederation. In the next selections, three Virginians, Patrick Henry, William Grayson, and Richard Henry Lee assert that the condition of the nation was sound and the Confederation on the whole successful—a view held widely in other states. Historians have since lent some support to this view. The postwar depression was not the fault of the Confederation and the country began to recover before 1788. Moreover, for all its shortcomings, the Confederation successfully concluded the war on terms highly favorable to the United States: it established the first national bureaucracy, formulated liberal policies for the disposal of the public domain and the creation of new states in the West, and paid the interest on the foreign debt.

Despite these accomplishments, George Washington spoke for many leaders when he wrote in 1787: "To be more exposed in the eyes of the world, and more contemptible than we already are, is hardly possible." Washington therefore felt obliged to attend and preside over the Philadelphia Convention called by Congress to amend the Articles. Previous attempts to enlarge the powers of Congress by granting it authority to levy taxes and regulate interstate and foreign commerce had foundered on state rivalries and the necessity to get unanimous approval of any changes. People were afraid to entrust greater power to the Confederation because the Articles, which had created a weak government, contained no mechanisms for preventing the misuse of power. Devising such mechanisms to balance power against power and to protect various interests became the principle job of the Philadelphia Convention whose performance is appraised in the selection by John P. Roche. Roche argues that the founding fathers were radical revolutionaries as well as practical politicians. They drafted a document that they thought would meet with popular approval but that would also remedy the defects of the Union.

CONFLICTING VIEWS OF THE ARTICLES OF CONFEDERATION

6 FROM   *James Madison*
Vices of the Political System of the United States

Failure of the States to Comply with the Constitutional Requisitions. This evil has been so fully experienced both during the war and since the peace, results so naturally from the number and independent authority of the States, and has been so uniformly exemplified in every similar Confederacy, that it may be considered as not less radically and permanently inherent in, than it is fatal to the object of, the present system.

Encroachments by the States on the Federal Authority. Examples of this are numerous, and repetitions may be foreseen in almost every case where any favorite object of a State shall present a temptation. Among these examples are the wars and treaties of Georgia with the Indians, the unlicensed compacts between Virginia and Maryland and between Pennsylvania and New Jersey, the troops raised and to be kept up by Massachusetts.

Violations of the Law of Nations and of Treaties. From the number of Legislatures, the sphere of life from which most of their members are taken, and the circumstances under which their legislative business is carried on, irregularities of this kind must frequently happen. Accordingly, not a year has passed without instances of them in some one or other of the States. The Treaty of Peace, the treaty with France, the treaty with Holland,

SOURCE: James Madison, "Vices of the Political System of the United States," in *Letters and Other Writings of James Madison*, I, pp. 319–328 (Philadelphia: Lippincott, 1867).

have each been violated. [See the complaints to Congress on these subjects.] The causes of these irregularities must necessarily produce frequent violations of the law of nations in other respects.

As yet, foreign powers have not been rigorous in animadverting on us. This moderation, however, cannot be mistaken for a permanent partiality to our faults, or a permanent security against those disputes with other nations, which, being among the greatest of public calamities, it ought to be least in the power of any part of the community to bring on the whole.

Trespasses of the States on the Right of Each Other. These are alarming symptoms, and may be daily apprehended, as we are admonished by daily experience. See the law of Virginia restricting foreign vessels to certain ports; of Maryland in favor of vessels belonging to her *own citizens;* of N. York in favor of the same.

Paper money, instalments of debts, occlusion of courts, making property a legal tender, may likewise be deemed aggressions on the rights of other States. As the citizens of every State, aggregately taken, stand more or less in the relation of creditors or debtors to the citizens of every other State, acts of the debtor State in favor of debtors affect the creditor State in the same manner as they do its own citizens, who are, relatively creditors towards other citizens. This remark may be extended to foreign nations. If the exclusive regulation of the value and alloy of coin was properly delegated to the federal authority, the policy of it equally requires a controul on the States in the cases above mentioned. It must have been meant—1. To preserve uniformity in the circulating medium throughout the nation. 2. To prevent those frauds on the citizens of other States, and the subjects of foreign powers, which might disturb the tranquillity at home, or involve the union in foreign contests.

The practice of many States in restricting the commercial intercourse with other States, and putting their productions and manufactures on the same footing with those of foreign nations, though not contrary to the federal articles, is certainly adverse to the spirit of the Union, and tends to beget retaliating regulations, not less expensive and vexatious in themselves than they are destructive of the general harmony.

Want of Concert in Matters Where Common Interest Requires it. This defect is strongly illustrated in the state of our commercial affairs. How much has the national dignity, interest, and revenue, suffered from this cause? Instances of inferior moment are the want of uniformity in the laws concerning naturalization and literary property; of provision for national seminaries; for grants of incorporation for national purposes, for canals, and other works of general utility; which may at present be defeated by the perverseness of particular States whose concurrence is necessary. . . .

Want of Sanction to the Laws, and of Coercion in the Government of the Confederacy. A sanction is essential to the idea of law, as coercion is to that of Government. The federal system being destitute of both, wants the great vital principles of a Political Constitution. Under the form of such a Constitution, it is in fact nothing more than a treaty of amity, of commerce, and of alliance, between independent and Sovereign States. From what cause could so fatal an omission have happened in the articles of Confederation? From a mistaken confidence that the justice, the good faith, the honor, the sound policy of the several legislative assemblies would render superfluous any appeal to the ordinary motives by which the laws secure the obedience of individuals; a confidence which does honor to the enthusiastic virtue of the compilers, as much as the inexperience of the crisis apologizes for their errors. The time which has since elapsed has had the double effect of increasing the light and tempering the warmth with which the arduous work may be revised. It is no longer doubted that a unanimous and punctual obedience of 13 independent bodies to the acts of the federal Government ought not to be calculated on. Even during the war, when external danger supplied in some degree the defect of legal and coercive sanctions, how imperfectly did the States fulfil their obligations to the Union? In time of peace we see already what is to be expected. How, indeed, could it be otherwise? In the first place, every general act of the Union must necessarily bear unequally hard on some particular member or members of it; secondly, the partiality of the members to their own interests and rights, a partiality which will be fostered by the courtiers of popularity, will naturally exaggerate the inequality where it exists, and even suspect it where it has no existence; thirdly, a distrust of the voluntary compliance of each other may prevent the compliance of any, although it should be the latent disposition of all. Here are causes and pretexts which will never fail to render federal measures abortive. If the laws of the States were merely recommendatory to their citizens, or if they were to be rejudged by county authorities, what security, what probability would exist that they would be carried into execution? Is the security or probability greater in favor of the acts of Congress, which, depending for their execution on the will of the State legislatures, are, tho' nominally authoritative, in fact recommendatory only?

Want of Ratification by the People of the Articles of Confederation. In some of the States the Confederation is recognized by and forms a part of the Constitution. In others, however, it has received no other sanction than that of the legislative authority. From this defect two evils result: 1. Whenever a law of a State happens to be repugnant to an act of Congress, particularly when the latter is of posterior date to the former, it will be at least questionable whether the latter must not prevail; and as the question must be decided by the Tribunals of the State, they will be most likely to lean on the side of the State.

2. As far as the union of the States is to be regarded as a league of sovereign powers, and not as a political Constitution, by virtue of which they are become one sovereign power, so far it seems to follow, from the doctrine of compacts, that a breach of any of the articles of the Confederation by any of the parties to it absolves the other parties from their respective obligations, and gives them a right, if they choose to exert it, of dissolving the Union altogether.

Multiplicity of Laws in the Several States. In developing the evils which viciate the political system of the United States, it is proper to include those which are found within the States individually, as well as those which directly affect the States collectively, since the former class have an indirect influence on the general malady, and must not be overlooked in forming a compleat remedy. Among the evils, then, of our situation, may well be ranked the multiplicity of laws, from which no State is exempt. . . .

Injustice of the Laws of the States. If the multiplicity and mutability of laws prove a want of wisdom, their injustice betrays a defect still more alarming; more alarming, not merely because it is a greater evil in itself, but because it brings more into question the fundamental principle of republican Government, that the majority who rule in such Governments are the safest guardians both of public good and of private rights. To what causes is this evil to be ascribed?

These causes lie—1. In the representative bodies. 2. In the people themselves.

1. Representative appointments are sought from 3 motives: 1. Ambition. 2. Personal interest. 3. Public good. Unhappily, the two first are proved by experience to be most prevalent. Hence, the candidates who feel them, particularly the second, are most industrious and most successful in pursuing their object; and forming often a majority in the legislative Councils, with interested views, contrary to the interest and views of their constituents, join in a perfidious sacrifice of the latter to the former. A succeeding election, it might be supposed, would displace the offenders, and repair the mischief. But how easily are base and selfish measures masked by pretexts of public good and apparent expediency? How frequently will a repetition of the same arts and industry which succeeded in the first instance again prevail on the unwary to misplace their confidence?

How frequently, too, will the honest but unenlightened representative be the dupe of a favorite leader, veiling his selfish views under the professions of public good, and varnishing his sophistical arguments with the glowing colours of popular eloquence?

2. A still more fatal, if not more frequent cause, lies among the people themselves. All civilized societies are divided into different interests and factions, as they happen to be creditors or debtors, rich or poor, husbandmen, merchants, or manufacturers, members of different religious sects, followers of different political leaders, inhabitants of different districts, owners of different kinds of property, &c., &c. In republican Government, the majority, however composed, ultimately give the law. Whenever, therefore, an apparent interest or common passion unites a majority, what is to restrain them from unjust violations of the rights and interests of the minority, or individuals? Three motives only: 1.

A prudent regard to their own good, as involved in the general and permanent good of the community. This consideration, although of decisive weight in itself, is found by experience to be too often unheeded. It is too often forgotten, by nations as well as by individuals, that honesty is the best policy. 2dly. Respect for character. However strong this motive may be in individuals, it is considered as very insufficient to restrain them from injustice. In a multitude its efficacy is diminished in proportion to the number which is to share the praise or the blame. Besides, as it has reference to public opinion, which, within a particular society is the opinion of the majority, the standard is fixed by those whose conduct is to be measured by it. The public opinion without the society will be little respected by the people at large of any Country. Individuals of extended views and of national pride may bring the public proceedings to this standard, but the example will never be followed by the multitude. Is it to be imagined that an ordinary citizen or even Assemblyman of R. Island, in estimating the policy of paper money, ever considered or cared in what light the measure would be viewed in France or Holland, or even in Massachusetts or Connecticut? It was a sufficient temptation to both that it was for their interest; it was a sufficient sanction to the latter that it was popular in the State; to the former, that it was so in the neighbourhood. 3dly. Will Religion, the only remaining motive, be a sufficient restraint? It is not pretended to be such, on men individually considered. Will its effect be greater on them considered in an aggregate view? Quite the reverse. The conduct of every popular assembly acting on oath, the strongest of religious ties, proves that individuals join without remorse in acts against which their consciences would revolt if proposed to them under the like sanction, separately, in their closets. When, indeed, Religion is kindled into enthusiasm, its force, like that of other passions, is increased by the sympathy of a multitude. But enthusiasm is only a temporary state of religion, and, while it lasts, will hardly be seen with pleasure at the helm of Government. Besides, as religion in its coolest state is not infallible, it may become a motive to oppression as well as a restraint from injustice. Place three individuals in a situation wherein the interest of each depends on the voice of the others, and give to two of them an interest opposed to the rights of the third. Will the latter be secure? The prudence of every man would shun the danger. The rules and forms of justice suppose and guard against it. Will two thousand in a like situation be less likely to encroach on the rights of one thousand? The contrary is witnessed by the notorious factions and oppressions which take place in corporate towns, limited as the opportunities are, and in little republics, when uncontrouled by apprehensions of external danger. If an enlargement of the sphere is found to lessen the insecurity of private rights, it is not because the impulse of a common interest or passion is less predominant in this case with the majority, but because a common interest or passion is less apt to be felt, and the requisite combinations less easy to be formed, by a great than by a small number. The society becomes broken into a greater variety of interests and pursuits of passions, which check each other, whilst those who may feel a common sentiment have less opportunity of communication and concert. It may be inferred that the inconveniences of popular States, contrary to the prevailing Theory, are in proportion not to the extent, but to the narrowness of their limits.

The great desideratum in Government is such a modification of the sovereignty as will render it sufficiently neutral between the different interests and factions to controul one part of the society from invading the rights of another, and, at the same time, sufficiently controuled itself from setting up an interest adverse to that of the whole society. In absolute Monarchies the prince is sufficiently neutral towards his subjects, but frequently sacrifices their happiness to his ambition or his avarice. In small Republics, the sovereign will is sufficiently controuled from such a sacrifice of the entire Society, but is not sufficiently neutral towards the parts composing it. As a limited monarchy tempers the evils of an absolute one, so an extensive Republic meliorates the administration of a small Republic.

An auxiliary desideratum for the melioration of the Republican form is such a process of elections as will most certainly extract from the mass of the society the purest and noblest characters which it contains; such as will at once feel most strongly the proper motives to pursue the end of their appointment, and be most capable to devise the proper means of attaining it.

VIRTUES OF THE POLITICAL SYSTEM OF THE UNITED STATES

7 FROM   *Patrick Henry*
The Virginia Convention

Consider our situation, sir: go to the poor man, and ask him what he does. He will inform you that he enjoys the fruits of his labor, under his own fig-tree, with his wife and children around him, in peace and security. Go to every other member of society,—you will find the same tranquil ease and content; you will find no alarms or disturbances. Why, then, tell us of danger, to terrify us into an adoption of this new form of government? And yet who knows the dangers that this new system may produce? They are out of the sight of the common people: they cannot foresee latent consequences. I dread the operation of it on the middling and lower classes of people: it is for them I fear the adoption of this system.

SOURCE: Patrick Henry in Jonathan Elliot, Comp., *The Debates in the Several State Conventions on the Adoption of the Federal Constitution as Recommended by the General Convention at Philadelphia*, 2nd ed., III, p. 54 (Philadelphia: Lippincott, 1896).

8   FROM   *William Grayson*
                 The Virginia Convention

. . . I beg leave to consider the circumstances of the Union
antecedent to the meeting of the Convention at Philadelphia.
We have been told of phantoms and ideal dangers to lead us into
measures which will, in my opinion, be the ruin of our country.
If the existence of those dangers cannot be proved, if there be no
apprehension of wars, if there be no rumors of wars, it will place
the subject in a different light, and plainly evince to the world that
there cannot be any reason for adopting measures which we
apprehend to be ruinous and destructive. When this state proposed that the general government should be improved, Massachusetts was just recovered from a rebellion which had brought
the republic to the brink of destruction—from a rebellion which
was crushed by that federal government which is now so much
contemned and abhorred: a vote of that august body for fifteen
hundred men, aided by the exertions of the state, silenced all
opposition, and shortly restored the public tranquillity. Massachusetts was satisfied that these internal commotions were so
happily settled, and was unwilling to risk any similar distresses
by theoretic experiments. Were the Eastern States willing to
enter into this measure? Were they willing to accede to the proposal of Virginia? In what manner was it received? Connecticut
revolted at the idea. The Eastern States, sir, were unwilling to
recommend a meeting of a convention. They were well aware
of the dangers of revolutions and changes. Why was every effort
used, and such uncommon pains taken, to bring it about? This
would have been unnecessary, had it been approved of by the
people. Was Pennsylvania disposed for the reception of this
project of reformation? No, sir. She was even unwilling to amend
her revenue laws, so as to make the five per centum operative

SOURCE: William Grayson in Jonathan Elliot, Comp., *The Debates in the
Several State Conventions on the Adoption of the Federal Constitution as
Recommended by the General Convention at Philadelphia*, 2nd ed., III, pp.
274–276 (Philadelphia: Lippincott, 1896).

her revenue laws, so as to make the five per centum operative. She was satisfied with things as they were. There was no complaint, that ever I heard of, from any other part of the Union, except Virginia. This being the case among ourselves, what dangers were there to be apprehended from foreign nations? It will be easily shown that dangers from that quarter were absolutely imaginary. Was not France friendly? Unequivocally so. She was devising new regulations of commerce for our advantage. Did she harass us with applications for her money? Is it likely that France will quarrel with us? Is it not reasonable to suppose that she will be more desirous than ever to cling, after losing the Dutch republic, to her best ally? How are the Dutch? We owe them money, it is true; and are they not willing that we should owe them more? Mr. Adams applied to them for a new loan to the poor, despised Confederation. They readily granted it. The Dutch have a fellow-feeling for us. They were in the same situation with ourselves. . . .

The domestic debt is diminished by considerable sales of western lands to Cutler, Sergeant, and Company; to Simms; and to Royal, Flint, and Company. The board of treasury is authorized to sell in Europe, or any where else, the residue of those lands.

An act of Congress has passed, to adjust the public debts between the individual states and the United States.

Was our trade in a despicable situation? I shall say nothing of what did not come under my own observation. When I was in Congress, sixteen vessels had had sea letters in the East India trade, and two hundred vessels entered and cleared out, in the French West India Islands, in one year.

I must confess that public credit has suffered, and that our public creditors have been ill used. This was owing to a fault at the head-quarters,—to Congress themselves,—in not apportioning the debts on the different states, and in not selling the western lands at an earlier period. If requisitions have not been complied with, it must be owing to Congress, who might have put the unpopular debts on the back lands. Commutation is abhorrent to New England ideas. Speculation is abhorrent to the Eastern States. Those inconveniences have resulted from the bad policy of Congress.

9 FROM   *Richard Henry Lee*
   Letters from the Federal Farmer to the Republican

. . . If we remain cool and temperate, we are in no immediate danger of any commotions; we are in a state of perfect peace, and in no danger of invasions; the state governments are in the full exercise of their powers; and our governments answer all present exigencies, except the regulation of trade, securing credit, in some cases, and providing for the interest, in some instances, of the public debts; and whether we adopt a change three or nine months hence, can make but little odds with the private circumstances of individuals; their happiness and prosperity, after all, depend principally upon their own exertions. We are hardly recovered from a long and distressing war: The farmers, fishermen, &c. have not fully repaired the waste made by it. Industry and frugality are again assuming their proper station. Private debts are lessened, and public debts incurred by the war have been, by various ways, diminished; and the public lands have now become a productive source for diminishing them much more. I know uneasy men, who with very much to precipitate, do not admit all these facts; but they are facts well known to all men who are thoroughly informed in the affairs of this country. It must, however, be admitted, that our federal system is defective, and that some of the state governments are not well administered; but, then, we impute to the defects in our governments many evils and embarrassments which are most clearly the result of the late war. We must allow men to conduct on the present occasion, as on all similar one's. They will urge a thousand pretences to answer their purposes on both sides. When we want a man to change his condition, we describe it as wretched, miserable, and despised; and draw a pleasing picture of that which we would have him assume. And when we wish the contrary, we reverse our descriptions. Whenever a clamor is raised, and idle men get to

SOURCE: Richard Henry Lee, "Letters from the Federal Farmer to the Republican," in P. L. Ford, Ed., *Pamphlets on the Constitution of the United States*, pp. 280–281 (New York: Brooklyn Historical Printing Club, 1888).

descriptions. Whenever a clamor is raised, and idle men get to work, it is highly necessary to examine facts carefully, and without unreasonably suspecting men of falsehood, to examine, and enquire attentively, under what impressions they act. It is too often the case in political concerns that men state facts not as they are, but as they wish them to be; and almost every man, by calling to mind past scenes, will find this to be true.

FRAMING A NEW CONSTITUTION

10 FROM   *John P. Roche*
The Founding Fathers: A Reform Caucus in Action

Over the last century and a half, the work of the Constitutional
Convention and the motives of the Founding Fathers have been
analyzed under a number of different ideological auspices. To
one generation of historians, the hand of God was moving in the
assembly; under a later dispensation, the dialectic (at various
levels of philosophical sophistication) replaced the Deity: "relationships of production" moved into the niche previously
reserved for Love of Country. Thus in counterpoint to the Zeitgeist, the Framers have undergone miraculous metamorphoses:
at one time acclaimed as liberals and bold social engineers, today
they appear in the guise of sound Burkean conservatives, men
who in our time would subscribe to *Fortune,* look to Walter
Lippmann for political theory, and chuckle patronizingly at the
antics of Barry Goldwater. . . .

The "Fathers" have thus been admitted to our best circles; the
revolutionary ferocity which confiscated all Tory property in
reach and populated New Brunswick with outlaws has been
converted by the "Miltown School" of American historians into
a benign dedication to "consensus" and "prescriptive rights."
The Daughters of the American Revolution have, through the

SOURCE: John P. Roche, "The Founding Fathers: A Reform Caucus in
Action," in *American Political Science Review,* LV, pp. 799–816 (Dec. 1961).
Reprinted by permission of the American Political Science Association and
the author.

ministrations of Professors Boorstin, Hartz, and Rossiter, at last found ancestors worthy of their descendants. It is not my purpose here to argue that the "Fathers" were, in fact, radical revolutionaries; that proposition has been brilliantly demonstrated by Robert R. Palmer in his *Age of the Democratic Revolution*. My concern is with the further position that not only were they revolutionaries, but also they were democrats. Indeed, in my view, there is one fundamental truth about the Founding Fathers that *every* generation of Zeitgeisters has done its best to obscure: they were first and foremost superb democratic politicians. . . . They were, with their colleagues, *political men*—not metaphysicians disembodied conservatives or Agents of History—and as recent research into the nature of American politics in the 1780s confirms, they were committed (perhaps willy-nilly) to working within the democratic framework, within a universe of public approval. Charles Beard *and* the filiopietists to the contrary notwithstanding, the Philadelphia Convention was not a College of Cardinals or a council of Platonic guardians working within a manipulative, predemocratic framework; it was a *nationalist* reform caucus which had to operate with great delicacy and skill in a political cosmos full of enemies to achieve the one definitive goal—popular approbation.

Perhaps the time has come, to borrow Walton Hamilton's fine phrase, to raise the Framers from immortality to mortality, to give them credit for their magnificent demonstration of the art of democratic politics. The point must be reemphasized; they *made* history and did it within the limits of consensus. There was nothing inevitable about the future in 1787; the *Zeitgeist,* that fine Hegelian technique of begging causal questions, could only be discerned in retrospect. What they did was to hammer out a pragmatic compromise which would both bolster the "National interest" and be acceptable to the people. What inspiration they got came from their collective experience as professional politicians in a democratic society. As John Dickinson put it to his fellow delegates on August 13, "Experience must be our guide. Reason may mislead us."

In this context, let us examine the problems they confronted and the solutions they evolved. The Convention has been described picturesquely as a counter-revolutionary junta and the

Constitution as a *coup d'etat,* but this has been accomplished by withdrawing the whole history of the movement for constitutional reform from its true context. No doubt the goals of the constitutional elite were "subversive" to the existing political order, but it is overlooked that their subversion could only have succeeded if the people of the United States endorsed it by regularized procedures. Indubitably they were "plotting" to establish a much stronger central government than existed under the Articles, but only in the sense in which one could argue equally well that John F. Kennedy was, from 1956 to 1960, "plotting" to become President. In short, on the fundamental *procedural* level, the Constitutionalists had to work according to the prevailing rules of the game. Whether they liked it or not is a topic for spiritualists—and is irrelevant: one may be quite certain that had Washington agreed to play the De Gaulle (as the Cincinnati once urged), Hamilton would willingly have held his horse, but such fertile speculation in no way alters the actual context in which events took place.

I

When the Constitutionalists went forth to subvert the Confederation, they utilized the mechanisms of political legitimacy. And the roadblocks which confronted them were formidable. At the same time, they were endowed with certain potent political assets. The history of the United States from 1786 to 1790 was largely one of a masterful employment of political expertise by the Constitutionalists as against bumbling, erratic behavior by the opponents of reform. Effectively, the Constitutionalists had to induce the states, by democratic techniques of coercion, to emasculate themselves. To be specific, if New York had refused to join the new Union, the project was doomed; yet before New York was safely in, the reluctant state legislature had *sua sponte* to take the following steps: (1) agree to send delegates to the Philadelphia Convention; (2) provide maintenance for these delegates (these were distinct stages: New Hampshire was early in naming delegates, but did not provide for their maintenance until July); (3) set up the special *ad hoc* convention to decide on ratification; and (4) concede to the decision of the *ad hoc* convention that New York should participate. New York admittedly was a tricky state, with a strong interest in a *status quo* which permitted her to exploit New Jersey and Connecticut, but the same legal hurdles existed in every state. And at the risk of becoming boring, it must be reiterated that the *only* weapon in the Constitutionalist arsenal was an effective mobilization of public opinion.

The group which undertook this struggle was an interesting amalgam of a few dedicated nationalists with the self-interested spokesmen of various parochial bailiwicks. The Georgians, for example, wanted a strong central authority to provide military protection for their huge, underpopulated state against the Creek Confederacy; Jerseymen and Connecticuters wanted to escape from economic bondage to New York; the Virginians hoped to establish a system which would give that great state its rightful place in the councils of the republic. The dominant figures in the politics of these states therefore cooperated in the call for the Convention. In other states, the thrust towards national reform was taken up by opposition groups who added the "national interest" to their weapons system; in Pennsylvania, for instance, the group fighting to revise the Constitution of 1776 came out four-square behind the Constitutionalists, and in New York, Hamilton and the Schuyler *ambiance* took the same tack against George Clinton. There was, of course, a large element of personality in the affair: there is reason to suspect that Patrick Henry's opposition to the Convention and the Constitution was founded on his conviction that Jefferson was behind both, and a close study of local politics elsewhere would surely reveal that others supported the Constitution for the simple (and politically quite sufficient) reason that the "wrong" people were against it.

To say this is not to suggest that the Constitution rested on a foundation of impure or base motives. It is rather to argue that in politics there are no immaculate conceptions, and that in the drive for a stronger general government, motives of all sorts played a part. Few men in the history of mankind have espoused a view of the "common good" or "public interest" that militated against their private status; even Plato with all his reverence for disembodied reason managed to put philosophers on top of the pile. Thus it is not surprising that a number of diversified private interests joined to push the nationalist public interest; what would have been surprising was the absence of such a pragmatic united front. And the fact remains that, however motivated, these men did demonstrate a willingness to compromise their parochial interests in behalf of an ideal which took shape before their eyes and under their ministrations.

As Stanley Elkins and Eric McKitrick have suggested in a perceptive essay, what distinguished the leaders of the Constitutionalist caucus from their enemies was a "Continental" approach to political, economic and military issues. To the extent that they shared an institutional base of operations, it was the Continental Congress (thirty-nine of the delegates to the Federal Convention had served in Congress) , and this was hardly a locale which inspired respect for the state governments. Robert de Jouvenal observed French politics half a century ago and noted that a revolutionary Deputy had more in common with a non-revolutionary Deputy than he had with a revolutionary non-Deputy; similarly one can surmise that membership in the Congress under the Articles of Confederation worked to establish a continental frame of reference, that a Congressman from Pennsylvania and one from South Carolina would share a universe of discourse which provided them with a conceptual common denominator *vis à vis* their respective state legislatures. This was particularly true with respect to external affairs: the average state legislator was probably about as concerned with foreign policy then as he is today, but Congressmen were constantly forced to take the broad view of American prestige, were compelled to listen to the reports of Secretary John Jay and to the dispatches and pleas from their frustrated envoys in Britain, France and Spain. From considerations such as these, a "Continental" ideology developed which seems to have demanded a revision of our domestic institutions primarily on the ground that only by invigorating our general government could we assume our rightful place in the international arena. Indeed, an argument with great force—particularly since Washington was its incarnation—urged that our very survival in the Hobbesian jungle of world politics depended upon a reordering and strengthening of our national sovereignty.

Note that I am not enclosing the "Critical Period" thesis; on the contrary, Merrill Jensen seems to me quite sound in his view that for most Americans, engaged as they were in self-sustaining agriculture, the "Critical Period" was not particularly critical. In fact, the great achievement of the Constitutionalists was their ultimate success in convincing the elected representatives of a majority of the white male population that change was imperative. A small group of political leaders with a Continental vision and essentially a consciousness of the United States' *international* impotence, provided the matrix of the movement. To their standard other leaders rallied with their own parallel ambitions. Their great assets were (1) the presence in their caucus of the one authentic American "father figure," George Washington, whose prestige was enormous, (2) the energy and talent of their leadership (in which one must include the towering intellectuals of the time, John Adams and Thomas Jefferson, despite their absence abroad), and their communications "network," which was far superior to anything on the opposition side; (3) the preemptive skill which made "their" issue The Issue and kept the locally oriented opposition permanently on the defensive; and (4) the subjective consideration that these men were spokesmen of a new and compelling credo: *American* nationalism, that ill-defined but nonetheless potent sense of collective purpose that emerged from the American Revolution.

Despite great institutional handicaps, the Constitutionalists managed in the mid-1780s to mount an offensive which gained momentum as years went by. Their greatest problem was lethargy, and paradoxically, the number of barriers in their path may have proved an advantage in the long run. Beginning with the initial battle to get the Constitutional Convention called and delegates appointed, they could never relax, never let up the pressure. In practical terms, this meant that the local "organizations" created by the Constitutionalists were perpetually in movement building up their cadres for the next fight. (The word organization has to be used with great caution: a political organization in the United States—as in contemporary England—generally consisted of a magnate and his following, or a coalition of magnates. This did not necessarily mean that it was "undemocratic" or "aristocratic," in the Aristotelian sense of the word:

while a few magnates such as the Livingstons could draft their followings, most exercised their leadership without coercion on the basis of popular endorsement. The absence of organized opposition did not imply the impossibility of competition any more than low public participation in elections necessarily indicated an undemocratic suffrage.)

The Constitutionalists got the jump on the "opposition" (a collective noun: oppositions would be more correct) at the outset with the demand for a Convention. Their opponents were caught in an old political trap: they were not being asked to approve any specific program of reform, but only to endorse a meeting to discuss and recommend needed reforms. If they took a hard line at the first stage, they were put in the position of glorifying the *status quo* and of denying the needs for *any* changes. Moreover, the Constitutionalists could go to the people with a persuasive argument for "fair play"— "How can you condemn reform before you know precisely what is involved?" Since the state legislatures obviously would have the final say on any proposals that might emerge from the Convention, the Constitutionalists were merely reasonable men asking for a chance. Besides, since they did not make any concrete proposals at that stage, they were in a position to capitalize on every sort of generalized discontent with the Confederation.

Perhaps because of their poor intelilgence system, perhaps because of over-confidence generated by the failure of all previous efforts to alter the Articles, the opposition awoke too late to the dangers that confronted them in 1787. Not only did the Constitutionalists manage to get every state but Rhode Island (where politics was enlivened by a party system reminiscent of the "Blues" and the "Greens" in the Byzantine Empire) to appoint delegates to Philadelphia, but when the results were in, it appeared that they dominated the delegations. Given the apathy of the opposition, this was a natural phenomenon: in an ideologically nonpolarized political atmosphere those who get appointed to a special committee are likely to be the men who supported the movement for its creation. . . .

II

With delegations safely named, the focus shifted to Philadelphia. While waiting for a quorum to assemble, James Madison got busy and drafted the so-called Randolph or Virginia Plan
with the aid of the Virginia delegation. This was a political
master-stroke. Its consequence was that one business got underway, the framework of discussion was established on Madison's
terms. There was no interminable argument over agenda; instead the delegates took the Virginia Resolutions—"just for purposes of discussion"—as their point of departure. And along with
Madison's proposals, many of which were buried in the course of
the summer, went his major premise: a new start on a Constitution rather than piecemeal amendment. This was not necessarily revolutionary—a little exegesis could demonstrate that a
new Constitution might be formulated as "amendments" to the
Articles of Confederation—but Madison's proposal that this
"lump sum" amendment go into effect after approval by nine
states (the Articles required unanimous state approval for any
amendment) was thoroughly subversive.

Standard treatments of the Convention divide the delegates
into "nationalists" and "states'-righters" with various improvised
shadings ("moderate nationalists," etc.) , but these are *a posteriori* categories which obfuscate more than they clarify. What
is striking to one who analyzes the Convention as a case-study in
democratic politics is the lack of clear-cut ideological divisions in
the Convention. Indeed, I submit that the evidence—Madison's
Notes, the correspondence of the delegates, and debates on ratification—indicates that this was a remarkably homogeneous body
on the ideological level. . . .

Basic differences of opinion emerged, of course, but these were
not ideological; they were *structural.* If the so-called "states'-
rights" group had not accepted the fundamental purposes of the
Convention, they could simply have pulled out and by doing so
have aborted the whole enterprise. Instead of bolting, they re-
turned day after day to argue and to compromise. An interesting
symbol of this basic homogeneity was the initial agreement on
secrecy: these professional politicians did not want to become
prisoners of publicity; they wanted to retain that freedom of

maneuver which is only possible when men are not forced to take public stands in the preliminary stages of negotiation. . . .

Commentators on the Constitution who have read *The Federalist* in lieu of reading the actual debates have credited the Fathers with the invention of a sublime concept called "Federalism." Unfortunately *The Federalist* is probative evidence for only one proposition: that Hamilton and Madison were inspired propagandists with a genius for retrospective symmetry. Federalism, as the theory is generally defined, was an improvisation which was later promoted into a political theory. Experts on "federalism" should take to heart the advice of David Hume, who warned in his *Of the Rise and Progress of the Arts and Sciences* that ". . . there is no subject in which we must proceed with more caution than in [history], lest we assign causes which never existed and reduce what is merely contingent to stable and universal principles." In any event, the final balance in the Constitution between the states and the nation must have come as a great disappointment to Madison, while Hamilton's unitary views are too well known to need elucidation.

It is indeed astonishing how those who have glibly designated James Madison the "father" of Federalism have overlooked the solid body of fact which indicates that he shared Hamilton's quest for a unitary central government. To be specific, they have avoided examining the clear import of the Madison-Virginia Plan, and have disregarded Madison's dogged inch-by-inch retreat from the bastions of centralization. The Virginia Plan envisioned a unitary national government effectively freed from and dominant over the states. The lower house of the national legislature was to be elected directly by the people of the states with membership proportional to population. The upper house was to be selected by the lower and the two chambers would elect the executive and choose the judges. The national government would be thus cut completely loose from the states.

The structure of the general government was freed from state control in a truly radical fashion, but the scope of the authority of the national sovereign as Madison initially formulated it was breathtaking—it was a formulation worthy of the Sage of Malmesbury himself. The national legislature was to be empowered to disallow the acts of state legislatures, and the central government was vested, in addition to the powers of the nation under the Articles of Confederation, with plenary authority where ". . . the separate States are incompetent or in which the harmony of the United States may be interrupted by the exercise of individual legislation." Finally, just to lock the door against state intrusion, the national Congress was to be given the power to use military force on recalcitrant states. This was Madison's "model" of an ideal national government, though it later received little publicity in *The Federalist*.

The interesting thing was the reaction of the Convention to this militant program for a strong autonomous central government. Some delegates were startled, some obviously leery of so comprehensive a project of reform, but nobody set off any fireworks and nobody walked out. Moreover, in the two weeks that followed, the Virginia Plan received substantial endorsement *en principe*. . . .

The Virginia Plan may therefore be considered, in ideological terms, as the delegates' Utopia, but as the discussions continued and became more specific, many of those present began to have second thoughts. After all, they were not residents of Utopia or guardians in Plato's Republic who could simply impose a philosophical idea on subordinate strata of the population. They were practical politicians in a democratic society, and no matter what their private dreams might be, they had to take home an acceptable package and defend it—and their own political futures—against predictable attack. On June 14 the breaking point between dream and reality took place. Apparently realizing that under the Virginia Plan, Massachusetts, Virginia and Pennsylvania could virtually dominate the national government—and probably appreciating that to sell this program to "the folks back home" would be impossible—the delegates from the small states dug in their heels and demanded time for a consideration of alternatives. One gets a graphic sense of the inner politics from John Dickinson's reproach to Madison: "You see the consequences of pushing things too far. Some of the members from the small States wish for two branches in the General Legislature and are friends to a good National Government; but we would sooner submit to a foreign power than . . . be deprived of an equality of suffrage in both branches of the Legislature, and

thereby be thrown under the domination of the large States."
. . . Now the process of accommodation was put into action smoothly—and wisely, given the character and strength of the doubters. Madison had the votes, but this was one of those situations where the enforcement of mechanical majoritarianism could easily have destroyed the objectives of the majority: the Constitutionalists were in quest of a qualitative as well as a quantitative consensus. This was hardly from deference to local Quaker custom; it was a political imperative if they were to attain ratification.

III

According to the standard script, at this point the "states'-rights" group intervened in force behind the New Jersey Plan, which has been characteristically portrayed as a reversion to the *status quo* under the Articles of Confederation with but minor modifications. A careful examination of the evidence indicates that only in a marginal sense is this an accurate description. It is true that the New Jersey Plan put the states back into the institutional picture, but one could argue that to do so was a recognition of political reality rather than an affirmation of states'-rights. A serious case can be made that the advocates of the New Jersey Plan, far from being ideological addicts of states'-rights, intended to substitute for the Virginia Plan a system which would both retain strong national power and have a chance of adoption in the states. The leading spokesman for the project asserted quite clearly that his views were based more on counsels of expediency than on principle; said Paterson on June 16: "I came here not to speak my own sentiments, but the sentiments of those who sent me. Our object is not such a Government as may be best in itself, but such a one as our Constituents have authorized us to prepare, and as they will approve.". . .

This was a defense of political acumen, not of states-rights. In fact, Paterson's notes of his speech can easily be construed as an argument for attaining the substantive objectives of the Virginia Plan by a sound political route, *i.e.,* pouring the new wine in the old bottles. . . .

In other words, the advocates of the New Jersey Plan concentrated their fire on what they held to be the *political liabilities* of the Virginia Plan—which were matters of institutional structure—rather than on the proposed scope of national authority. Indeed, the Supremacy Clause of the Constitution first saw the light of day in Paterson's Sixth Resolution; the New Jersey Plan contemplated the use of military force to secure compliance with national law; and finally Paterson made clear his view that under either the Virginia or the New Jersey systems, the general government would ". . . act on individuals and not on states." From the states'-rights viewpoint, this was heresy: the fundament of that doctrine was the proposition that any central government had as its constituents the states, not the people, and could only reach the people through the agency of the state government.

Paterson then reopened the agenda of the Convention, but he did so within a distinctly nationalist framework. Paterson's position was one of favoring a strong central government in principle, but opposing one which in fact *put the big states in the saddle.* (The Virginia Plan, for all its abstract merits, did very well by Virginia.) . . .

IV

On Tuesday morning, June 19, the vacation was over. James Madison led off with a long, carefully reasoned speech analyzing the New Jersey Plan which, while intellectually vigorous in its criticisms, was quite conciliatory in mood. "The great difficulty," he observed, "lies in the affair of Representation; and if this could be adjusted, all others would be surmountable." (As events were to demonstrate, this diagnosis was correct. When he finished, a vote was taken on whether to continue with the Virginia Plan as the nucleus for a new constitution: seven states voted "Yes"; New York, New Jersey, and Delaware voted "No"; and Maryland, whose position often depended on which delegates happened to be on the floor, divided. Paterson, it seems, lost decisively; yet in a fundamental sense he and his allies had achieved their purpose: from that day onward, it could never be forgotten that the state governments loomed ominously in the background and that no verbal incantations could exorcise their power. Moreover, nobody bolted the convention: Paterson and his colleagues took their defeat in stride and set to work to modify the Virginia Plan, particularly with respect to its provisions on representation in the national legislature. . . . The process of compromise had begun.

For the next two weeks, the delegates circled around the problem of legislative representation. The Connecticut delegation appears to have evolved a possible compromise quite early in the debates, but the Virginians and particularly Madison (unaware that he would later be acclaimed as the prophet of "federalism") fought obdurately against providing for equal representation of states in the second chamber. There was a good deal of acrimony and at one point Benjamin Franklin—of all people—proposed the institution of a daily prayer; practical politicians in the gathering, however, were meditating more on the merits of a good committee than on the utility of Divine intervention. On July 2, the ice began to break when through a number of fortuitous events—and one that seems deliberate—the majority against equality of representation was converted into a dead tie. The Convention had reached the stage where it was "ripe" for a solution (presumably all the therapeutic speeches had been made), and the South Carolinians proposed a committee. . . .

There is a common rumor that the Framers divided their time between philosophical discussions of government and reading the classics in political theory. Perhaps this is as good a time as any to note that their concerns were highly practical, that they spent little time canvassing abstractions. A number of them had some acquaintance with the history of political theory (probably gained from reading John Adams' monumental compilation *A Defense of the Constitutions of Government,* the first volume of which appeared in 1786), and it was a poor rhetorician indeed who could not cite Locke, Montesquieu, or Harrington *in support* of a desired goal. Yet up to this point in the deliberations, no one had expounded a defense of states'-rights or the "separation of powers" on anything resembling a theoretical basis. It should be reiterated that the Madison model had no room either for the states or for the "separation of power": effectively *all* governmental power was vested in the national legislature. . . .

It would be tedious to continue a blow-by-blow analysis of the work of the delegates; the critical fight was over representation of the states and once the Connecticut Compromise was adopted on July 17, the Convention was over the hump.* Madison, James Wilson, and Gouverneur Morris of New York (who was there representing Pennsylvania!) fought the compromise all the way in a last-ditch effort to get a unitary state with parliamentary supremacy. But their allies deserted them and they demonstrated after their defeat the essentially opportunist character of their objections—using "opportunist" here in a non-pejorative sense, to indicate a willingness to swallow their objections and get on with the business. Moreover, once the compromise had carried (by five states to four, with one state divided), its advocates threw themselves vigorously into the job of strengthening the general government's substantive powers—as might have been predicted, indeed, from Paterson's early statements. It nourishes an increased respect for Madison's devotion to the art of politics, to realize that this dogged fighter could sit down six months later and prepare essays for *The Federalist* in contradiction to his basic convictions about the true course the Convention should have taken.

V

Two tricky issues will serve to illustrate the later process of accommodation. The first was the institutional position of the Executive. Madison argued for an executive chosen by the National Legislature and on May 29 this had been adopted with a provision that after his seven-year term was concluded, the chief magistrate should not be eligible for reelection. In late July this was reopened and for a week the matter was argued from several different points of view. A good deal of desultory speech-making ensued, but the gist of the problem was the opposition from two sources to election by the legislature. One group felt that the states should have a hand in the process; another small but influential circle urged direct election by the people. There were a

* [Editor's note.] The Connecticut Compromise gave each state an equal voice in the Senate and apportioned representatives in the lower house according to population.

number of proposals: election by the people, election by state governors, by electors chosen by state legislatures, by the National Legislature (James Wilson, perhaps ironically, proposed at one point that an Electoral College be chosen by lot from the National Legislature!), and there was some resemblance to three-dimensional chess in the dispute because of the presence of two other variables, length of tenure and reeligibility. Finally, after opening, reopening, and re-reopening the debate, the thorny problem was consigned to a committee for resolution.

The Brearley Committee on Postponed Matters was a superb aggregation of talent and its compromise on the Executive was a masterpiece of political improvisation. (The Electoral College, its creation, however, had little in its favor as an *institution*—as the delegates well appreciated.) The point of departure for all discussion about the presidency in the Convention was that in immediate terms, the problem was non-existent; in other words, everybody present knew that under any system devised, George Washington would be President. Thus they were dealing in the future tense and to a body of working politicians the merits of the Brearley proposal were obvious: everybody got a piece of cake. (Or to put it more academically, each viewpoint could leave the Convention and argue to its constituents that it had *really* won the day.) First, the state legislatures had the right to determine the mode of selection of the electors; second, the small states received a bonus in the Electoral College in the form of a guaranteed minimum of three votes while the big states got acceptance of the principle of proportional power; third, if the state legislatures agree (as six did in the first presidential election), the people could be involved directly in the choice of electors; and finally, if no candidate received a majority in the College, the right of decision passed to the National Legislature with each state exercising equal strength. . . .

This compromise was almost too good to be true, and the Framers snapped it up with little debate or controversy. No one seemed to think well of the College as an *institution;* indeed, what evidence there is suggests that there was an assumption that once Washingon had finished his tenure as President, the electors would cease to produce majorities and the chief executive would usually be chosen in the House. George Mason observed casually that the selection would be made in the House nineteen times in twenty and no one seriously disputed this point. The vital aspect of the Electoral College was that it got the Convention over the hurdle and protected everybody's interests. The future was left to cope with the problem of what to do with this Rube Goldberg mechanism.

In short, the Framers did not in their wisdom endow the United States with a College of Cardinals—the Electoral College was neither an exercise in applied Platonism nor an experiment in indirect government based on elitist distrust of the masses. It was merely a jerry-rigged improvisation which has subsequently been endowed with a high theoretical content. . . .

The second issue on which some substantial practical bargaining took place was slavery. The morality of slavery was, by design, not at issue; but in its other concrete aspects, slavery colored the arguments over taxation, commerce, and representation. The "Three-Fifths Compromise," that three-fifths of the slaves would be counted both for representation and for purposes of direct taxation (which was drawn from the past—it was a formula of Madison's utilized by Congress in 1783 to establish the basis of state contributions to the Confederation treasury) had allayed some Northern fears about Southern over-representation (no one then foresaw the trivial role that direct taxation would play in later federal financial policy), but doubts still remained. The Southerners, on the other hand, were afraid that Congressional control over commerce would lead to the exclusion of slaves or to their excessive taxation as imports. Moreover, the Southerners were disturbed over "navigation acts," *i.e.,* tariffs, or special legislation providing, for example, that exports be carried only in American ships; as a section depending upon exports, they wanted protection from the potential voracity of their commercial brethren of the Eastern states. To achieve this end, Mason and others urged that the Constitution include a proviso that navigation and commercial laws should require a two-thirds vote in Congress.

These problems came to a head in late August and, as usual, were handed to a committee in the hope that, in Gouverneur Morris' words, ". . . these things may form a bargain among the Northern and Southern states." The Committee reported its measures of reconciliation on August 25, and on August 29 the package was wrapped up and delivered. What occurred can best be described in George Mason's dour version (he anticipated Calhoun in his conviction that permitting navigation acts to pass by majority vote would put the South in economic bondage to the North—it was mainly on this ground that he refused to sign the Constitution):

"The Constitution as agreed to till a fortnight before the Convention rose was such a one as he would have set his hand and heart to. . . . [Until that time] The 3 New England States were constantly with us in all questions . . . so that it was these three States with the 5 Southern ones against Pennsylvania, Jersey and Delaware. With respect to the importation of slaves, [decision-making] was left to Congress. This disturbed the two Southern-most States who knew that Congress would immediately suppress the importation of slaves. Those two States therefore struck up a bargain with the three New England States. If they would join to admit slaves for some years, the two Southern-most States would join in changing the clause which required the ⅔ of the Legislature in any vote [on navigation acts]. It was done." . . .

VI

Drawing on their vast collective political experience, utilizing every weapon in the politician's arsenal, looking constantly over their shoulders at their constituents, the delegates put together a Constitution. It was a makeshift affair; some sticky issues (for example, the qualification of voters) they ducked entirely; others they mastered with that ancient instrument of political sagacity, studied ambiguity (for example, citizenship), and some they just overlooked. In this last category, I suspect, fell the matter of the power of the federal courts to determine the constitutionality of acts of Congress. When the judicial article was formulated (Article III of the Constitution), deliberations were still in the stage where the legislature was endowed with broad power under the Randolph formulation, authority which by its own terms was scarcely amenable to judicial review. In essence, courts could hardly determine when ". . . the separate States are incompetent or . . . the harmony of the United States may be interrupted"; the National Legislature, as critics pointed out, was free to define its own jurisdiction. Later the definition of legislative authority was changed into the form we know, a series of stipulated powers, *but the delegates never seriously reexamined the jurisdiction of the judiciary under this new limited formulation.* All arguments on the intention of the Framers in this matter are thus deductive and a *posteriori,* though some obviously make more sense than others.

The Framers were busy and distinguished men, anxious to get back to their families, their positions, and their constituents, not members of the French Academy devoting a lifetime to a dictionary. They were trying to do an important job, and do it in such a fashion that their handiwork would be acceptable to very diverse constituencies. No one was rhapsodic about the final document, but it was a beginning, a move in the right direction, and one they had reason to believe the people would endorse. In addition, since they had modified the impossible amendment provisions of the Articles (the requirement of unanimity which could always be frustrated by "Rogues Island") to one demanding approval by only three-quarters of the states, they seemed confident that gaps in the fabric which experience would reveal could be rewoven without undue difficulty.

So with a neat phrase introduced by Benjamin Franklin (but devised by Gouverneur Morris) which made their decision sound unanimous, and an inspired benediction by the Old Doctor urging doubters to doubt their own infallibility, the Constitution was accepted and signed. Curiously, Edmund Randolph, who had played so vital a role throughout, refused to sign, as did his fellow Virginian George Mason and Elbridge Gerry of Massachusetts. . . .

Madison, despite his reservations about the Constitution, was the campaign manager in ratification. His first task was to get the Congress in New York to light its own funeral pyre by approving the "amendments" to the Articles and sending them on to the state legislatures. Above all, momentum had to be maintained. The anti-Constitutionalists, now thoroughly alarmed and no novices in politics, realized that their best tactic was attrition rather than direct opposition. Thus they settled on a position expressing qualified approval but calling for a second Convention to remedy various defects (the one with the most demagogic appeal was the lack of a Bill of Rights). Madison knew that to accede to this demand would be equivalent to losing the battle, nor would he agree to conditional approval (despite wavering even by Hamilton). This was an all-or-nothing proposition: national salvation or national impotence with no intermediate positions possible. Unable to get congressional approval, he settled for second best: a unanimous resolution of Congress transmitting the Constitution to the states for whatever action they saw fit to take. The opponents then moved from New York and the Congress, where they had attempted to attach amendments and conditions, to the states for the final battle.

At first the campaign for ratification went beautifully: within eight months after the delegates set their names to the document, eight states had ratified. Only in Massachusetts had the result been close (187–168). Theoretically, a ratification by one more state convention would set the new government in motion, but in fact until Virginia and New York acceded to the new Union, the latter was a fiction. New Hampshire was the next to ratify; Rhode Island was involved in its characteristic political convulsions (the Legislature there sent the Constitution out to the towns for decision by popular vote and it got lost among a series of local issues); North Carolina's convention did not meet until July and then postposed a final decision. This is hardly the place for an extensive analysis of the conventions of New York and Virginia. Suffice it to say that the Constitutionalists clearly outmaneuvered their opponents, forced them into impossible political positions, and won both states narrowly. . . .

VII

. . . The Constitution, then, was not an apotheosis of "constitutionalism," a triumph of architectonic genius; it was a patch-work sewn together under the pressure of both time and events by a group of extremely talented democratic politicians. They refused to attempt the establishment of a strong, centralized sovereignty on the principle of legislative supremacy for the excellent reason that the people would not accept it. They risked their political fortunes by opposing the established doctrines of state sovereignty because they were convinced that the existing system was leading to national impotence and probably foreign domination. For two years, they worked to get a convention established. For over three months, in what must have seemed to the faithful participants an endless process of give-and-take, they reasoned, cajoled, threatened, and bargained amongst themselves. The result was a Constitution which the people, in fact, by democratic processes, did accept, and a new and far better national government was established.

Beginning with the inspired propaganda of Hamilton, Madison and Jay, the ideological build-up got under way. *The Federalist* had little impact on the ratification of the Constitution, except perhaps in New York, but this volume had enormous influence on the image of the Constitution in the minds of future generations, particularly on historians and political scientists who have an innate fondness for theoretical symmetry. Yet, while the shades of Locke and Montesquieu *may* have been hovering in the background, and the delegates *may* have been unconscious instruments of a transcendent *telos,* the careful observer of the day-to-day work of the Convention finds no over-arching principles. The "separation of powers" to him seems to be a by-product of suspicion, and "federalism" he views as a *pis aller,* as the farthest point the delegates felt they could go in the destruction of state power without themselves inviting repudiation.

To conclude, the Constitution was neither a victory for abstract theory nor a great practical success. Well over half a million men had to die on the battlefields of the Civil War before certain constitutional principles could be defined—a baleful consideration which is somehow overlooked in our customary tributes to the farsighted genius of the Framers and to the supposed American talent for "constitutionalism." The Constitution was, however, a vivid demonstration of effective democratic political action, and of the forging of a national elite which literally persuaded its countrymen to hoist themselves by their own boot straps. American pro-consuls would be wise not to translate the Constitution into Japanese, or Swahili, or treat it as a work of semi-Divine origin; but when students of comparative politics examine the process of nation-building in countries newly freed from colonial rule, they may find the American experience instructive as a classic example of the potentialities of a democratic elite.

PART FOUR

The Conflict over the Constitution

The Philadelphia Convention completed its work by September, 1787. For four months the founding fathers had struggled to devise a constitution that would improve the country's chances of resolving successfully the crises of national development that the young republic would confront in the ensuing decades. They created a strong central government but left extensive power to the states in an effort to strike a balance between the need for greater national integration and the necessity to respect parochial interests and attitudes. Similarly, they provided for direct popular participation in the election of the House of Representatives to give the new regime democratic legitimacy and to give citizens a share in decision making; they also restricted popular control through indirect election of the President and the Senate. The Convention labored in the knowledge that the Constitution would have to win public support.

The struggle over ratification by the states proved to be even fiercer than the disagreements within the secret conclaves of the convention itself. Each state elected delegates to a ratifying convention; six assented with little controversy but elsewhere, particularly in large and important states such as New York, Virginia, and Massachusetts, powerful opposition came close to defeating the Constitution.

The ratification process amounted to the first nationwide referendum in American history. It was the initial step in the development of a truly national political arena in which citizens, wherever they lived and whatever their particular interests and attitudes, regarded the Union as vitally affecting their interests. Some thought the proposed new government would promote their well-being, but others were unsure and still others perceived dangers to their interests. In 1911, Charles A. Beard (1874–1949), the leading American historian of his generation, published a provocative thesis that viewed the movement for the Constitution as a struggle between conflicting economic interests. In the course of developing a comprehensive economic interpretation of American history in which the dynamic role was played by rival classes such as merchants and capitalists, farmers and workers, Beard thought that the principal forces behind the Federal Constitution were merchants and public security holders who stood to benefit from a strong central government and the principal opposition came from farmers who stood to lose.

Though many of Beard's contemporaries regarded his thesis, which is reprinted below, as blasphemous because it attributed sordid motives to the glorified founding fathers, it eventually captured the minds and hearts of a whole generation of historians. Within the last twenty years, however, scholars have critically questioned the validity of Beard's economic interpretation, none more astringently and powerfully than Cecilia Kenyon who dissects Beard's thesis in the second selection below.

THE CONSTITUTION AND THE CONFLICT OF CLASSES

11 FROM   *Charles A. Beard*
An Economic Interpretation of the Constitution

. . . The weight of the several species of property in politics is not determined by the amount, but rather by the opportunities offered to each variety for gain and by the degree of necessity for defence against hostile legislation designed to depreciate values or close opportunities for increments. When viewed in this light the reason for the special pressure of personalty* in politics in 1787 is apparent. It was receiving attacks on all hands from the depreciators and it found the way to profitable operations closed by governmental action or neglect. If we may judge from the politics of the Congress under the Articles of Confederation, two related groups were most active: those working for the establishment of a revenue sufficient to discharge the interest and principal of the public debt, and those working for commercial regulations advantageous to personalty operations in shipping and manufacturing and in western land speculations.

It should be remembered also that personalty is usually more active than real property. It is centralized in the towns and can

---

* [Editor's note.] By personalty, Beard meant nonlanded forms of wealth, such as public securities and merchant shipping.

SOURCE: Charles A. Beard, *An Economic Interpretation of the Constitution*, pp. 50, 63, 73–74, 149–158, 217–218, 237–240, 251–252, 324–325 (New York: The Macmillan Co., 1913).

draw together for defence or aggression with greater facility. The expectation of profits from its manipulation was much larger in 1787 than from real property. It had a considerable portion of the professional classes attached to it; its influence over the press was tremendous, not only through ownership, but also through advertising and other patronage. It was, in short, the dynamic element in the movement for the new Constitution. . . .

Certain tentative conclusions emerge at this point.

Large and important groups of economic interests were adversely affected by the system of government under the Articles of Confederation, namely, those of public securities, shipping and manufacturing, money at interest; in short, capital as opposed to land.

The representatives of these important interests attempted through the regular legal channels to secure amendments to the Articles of Confederation which would safeguard their rights in the future, particularly those of the public creditors.

Having failed to realize their great purposes through the regular means, the leaders in the movement set to work to secure by a circuitous route the assemblying of a Convention to "revise" the Articles of Confederation with the hope of obtaining, outside of the existing legal framework, the adoption of a revolutionary programme.

Ostensibly, however, the formal plan of approval by Congress and the state legislatures was to be preserved.

Having shown that four groups of property rights were adversely affected by the government under the Articles of Confederation, and that economic motives were behind the movement for a reconstruction of the system, it is now necessary to inquire whether the members of the Convention which drafted the Constitution represented in their own property affiliations any or all of these groups. In other words, did the men who formulated the fundamental law of the land possess the kinds of property which were immediately and directly increased in value or made more secure by the results of their labors at Philadelphia? Did they have money at interest? Did they own public securities? Did they hold western lands for appreciation? Were they interested in shipping and manufactures?

The purpose of such an inquiry is not, of course, to show that the Constitution was made for the personal benefit of the members of the Convention. Far from it. Neither is it of any moment to discover how many hundred thousand dollars accrued to them as a result of the foundation of the new government. The only point here considered is: Did they represent distinct groups whose economic interests they understood and felt in concrete, definite form through their own personal experience with identical property rights, or were they working merely under the guidance of abstract principles of political science?

Unfortunately, the materials for such a study are very scanty, because the average biographer usually considers as negligible the processes by which his hero gained his livelihood. The pages which follow are, therefore, more an evidence of what ought to be done than a record of results actually accomplished. They would be meagre, indeed, were it not for the rich unpublished records of the Treasury Department which are here used for the first time in this connection; and they would doubtless have been fuller were it not for the fact that most of the books showing the central operations of the Treasury Department under Hamilton have disappeared. . . .

A survey of the economic interests of the members of the Convention presents certain conclusions:

A majority of the members were lawyers by profession.

Most of the members came from towns, on or near the coast, that is, from the regions in which personalty was largely concentrated.

Not one member represented in his immediate personal economic interests the small farming or mechanic classes.

The overwhelming majority of members, at least five-sixths, were immediately, directly, and personally interested in the outcome of their labors at Philadelphia, and were to a greater or less extent economic beneficiaries from the adoption of the Constitution.

1. Public security interests were extensively represented in the Convention. Of the fifty-five members who attended no less than forty appear on the Records of the Treasury Department for sums varying from a few dollars up to more than one hundred thousand dollars. . . .

It is interesting to note that, with the exception of New York, and possibly Delaware, each state had one or more prominent representatives in the Convention who held more than a negligible amount of securities, and who could therefore speak with feeling and authority on the question of providing in the new Constitution for the full discharge of the public debt. . . .

2. Personalty invested in lands for speculation was represented by at least fourteen members. . . .

3. Personalty in the form of money loaned at interest was represented by at least twenty-four members. . . .

4. Personalty in mercantile, manufacturing, and shipping lines was represented by at least eleven members. . . .

5. Personalty in slaves was represented by at least fifteen members. . . .

It cannot be said, therefore, that the members of the Convention were "disinterested." On the contrary, we are forced to accept the profoundly significant conclusion that they knew through their personal experiences in economic affairs the precise results which the new government that they were setting up was designed to attain. As a group of doctrinaires, like the Frankfort assembly of 1848, they would have failed miserably; but as practical men they were able to build the new government upon the only foundations which could be stable: fundamental economic interests.*

It is difficult for the superficial student of the Constitution, who has read only the commentaries of the legists, to conceive of that instrument as an economic document. It places no property qualifications on voters or officers; it gives no outward recognition of any economic groups in society; it mentions no special privileges to be conferred upon any class. It betrays no feeling, such as vibrates through the French constitution of 1791; its language is cold, formal, and severe.

The true inwardness of the Constitution is not revealed by an examination of its provisions as simple propositions of law; but by a long and careful study of the voluminous correspondence of

---

* The fact that a few members of the Convention, who had considerable economic interests at stake, refused to support the Constitution does not invalidate the general conclusions here presented. In the cases of Yates, Lansing, Luther Martin, and Mason, definite economic reasons for their action are forthcoming; but this is a minor detail.

the period, contemporary newspapers and pamphlets, the records of the debates in the Convention at Philadelphia and in the several state conventions, and particularly, *The Federalist,* which was widely circulated during the struggle over ratification. The correspondence shows the exact character of the evils which the Constitution was intended to remedy; the records of the proceedings in the Philadelphia Convention reveal the successive steps in the building of the framework of the government under the pressure of economic interests; the pamphlets and newspapers disclose the ideas of the contestants over the ratification; and *The Federalist* presents the political science of the new system as conceived by three of the profoundest thinkers of the period, Hamilton, Madison, and Jay. . . .

The Federalist . . . presents in a relatively brief and systematic form an economic interpretation of the Constitution by the men best fitted, through an intimate knowledge of the ideals of the framers, to expound the political science of the new government. This wonderful piece of argumentation by Hamilton, Madison, and Jay is in fact the finest study in the economic interpretation of politics which exists in any language; and whoever would understand the Constitution as an economic document need hardly go beyond it. It is true that the tone of the writers is somewhat modified on account of the fact that they are appealing to the voters to ratify the Constitution, but at the same time they are, by the force of circumstances, compelled to convince large economic groups that safety and strength lie in the adoption of the new system.

Indeed, every fundamental appeal in it is to some material and substantial interest. Sometimes it is to the people at large in the name of protection against invading armies and European coalitions. Sometimes it is to the commercial classes whose business is represented as prostrate before the follies of the Confederation. Now it is to creditors seeking relief against paper money and the assaults of the agrarians in general; now it is to the holders of federal securities which are depreciating toward the vanishing point. But above all, it is to the owners of personalty anxious to find a foil against the attacks of levelling democracy, that the authors of *The Federalist* address their most cogent arguments in favor of ratification. It is true there is much discussion of the details of the new frame-work of government, to which even some friends of reform took exceptions; but Madison and Hamilton both knew that these were incidental matters when compared with the sound basis upon which the superstructure rested.

In reading the pages of this remarkable work as a study in political economy, it is important to bear in mind that the system, which the authors are describing, consisted of two fundamental parts—one positive, the other negative:

I. A government endowed with certain positive powers, but so constructed as to break the force of majority rule and prevent invasions of the property rights of minorities.

II. Restrictions on the state legislatures which had been so vigorous in their attacks on capital.

Under some circumstances, action is the immediate interest of the dominant party; and whenever it desires to make an economic gain through governmental functioning, it must have, of course, a system endowed with the requisite powers. . . .

Before taking up the economic implications of the structure of the federal government, it is important to ascertain what, in the opinion of *The Federalist,* is the basis of all government. The most philosophical examination of the foundations of political science is made by Madison in the tenth number. Here he lays down, in no uncertain language, the principle that the first and elemental concern of every government is economic.

1. "The first object of government," he declares, is the protection of "the diversity in the faculties of men, from which the rights of property originate." The chief business of government, from which, perforce, its essential nature must be derived, consists in the control and adjustment of conflicting economic interests. After enumerating the various forms of propertied interests which spring up inevitably in modern society, he adds: "The regulation of these various and interfering interests forms the principal task of modern legislation, and involves the spirit of party and faction in the ordinary operations of the government."

2. What are the chief causes of these conflicting political forces with which the government must concern itself? Madison answers. Of course fanciful and frivolous distinctions have sometimes been the cause of violent conflicts; "but the most common and durable source of factions has been the various and unequal distribution

of property. Those who hold and those who are without property have ever formed distinct interests in society. Those who are creditors, and those who are debtors, fall under a like discrimination. A landed interest, a manufacturing interest, a mercantile interest, a moneyed interest, with many lesser interests grow up of necessity in civilized nations, and divide them into different classes actuated by different sentiments and views."

3. The theories of government which men entertain are emotional reactions to their property interests. "From the protection of different and unequal faculties of acquiring property, the possession of different degrees and kinds of property immediately results; *and from the influence of these on the sentiments and views of the respective proprietors, ensues a division of society into different interests and parties.*" Legislatures reflect these interests. "What," he asks, "are the different classes of legislators but advocates and parties to the causes which they determine." There is no help for it. "The causes of faction cannot be removed," and "we well know that neither moral nor religious motives can be relied on as an adequate control."

4. Unequal distribution of property is inevitable, and from it contending factions will rise in the state. The government will reflect them, for they will have their separate principles and "sentiments"; but the supreme danger will arise from the fusion of certain interests into an overbearing majority, which Madison, in another place, prophesied would be the landless proletariat,— an overbearing majority which will make its "rights" paramount, and sacrifice the "rights" of the minority. "To secure the public good," he declares, "and private rights against the danger of such a faction and at the same time preserve the spirit and the form of popular government is then the great object to which our inquiries are directed."

5. How is this to be done? Since the contending classes cannot be eliminated and their interests are bound to be reflected in politics, the only way out lies in making it difficult for enough contending interests to fuse into a majority, and in balancing one over against another. The machinery for doing this is created by the new Constitution and by the Union. *(a)* Public views are to be refined and enlarged "by passing them through the medium of a chosen body of citizens." *(b)* The very size of the Union will

enable the inclusion of more interests so that the danger of an overbearing majority is not so great. "The smaller the society, the fewer probably will be the distinct parties and interests composing it; the fewer the distinct parties and interests, the more frequently will a majority be found of the same party. . . . Extend the sphere, and you take in a greater variety of parties and interests; you make it less probable that a majority of the whole will have a common motive to invade the rights of other citizens; or if such a common motive exists, it will be more difficult for all who feel it to discover their strength and to act in unison with each other."

Q. E. D., "in the extent and proper structure of the Union, therefore, we behold a republican remedy for the diseases most incident to republican government."

On the 17th day of September, 1787, the Convention at Philadelphia finished its work and transmitted the new Constitution to Congress, with the suggestion that "it should afterwards be submitted to a convention of delegates chosen in each state by the people thereof, under the recommendation of its legislature for their assent and ratification; and that each convention assenting to and ratifying the same should give notice thereof to the United States in Congress assembled." The Philadelphia Convention further proposed that when nine states had ratified the new instrument, it should go into effect as between the states ratifying the same. Eleven days later, on September 28, the Congress, then sitting in New York, resolved to accept the advice of the Convention, and sent the Constitution to the state legislatures to be transmitted by them to conventions chosen by the voters of the respective commonwealths.

This whole process was a departure from the provisions of the then fundamental law of the land—the Articles of Confederation—which provided that all alterations and amendments should be made by Congress and receive the approval of the legislature of every state. If to-day the Congress of the United States should call a national convention to "revise" the Constitution, and such a convention should throw away the existing instrument of government entirely and submit a new frame of government to a popular referendum, disregarding altogether the process of amendment now provided, we should have something analogous to the great political transformation of 1787–89. The revolutionary nature of the work of the Philadelphia Convention is correctly characterized by Professor John W. Burgess when he states that had such acts been performed by Julius or Napoleon, they would have been pronounced *coups d'état*. . . .

A survey of the facts here presented yields several important generalizations:

Two states, Rhode Island and North Carolina refused to ratify the Constitution until after the establishment of the new government which set in train powerful economic forces against them in their isolation.

In three states, New Hampshire, New York, and Massachusetts, the popular vote as measured by the election of delegates to the conventions was adverse to the Constitution; and ratification was secured by the conversion of opponents and often the repudiation of their tacit (and in some cases express) instructions.

In Virginia the popular vote was doubtful.

In the four states which ratified the constitution with facility, Connecticut, New Jersey, Georgia, and Delaware, only four or five weeks were allowed to elapse before the legislatures acted, and four or five weeks more before the elections to the conventions were called; and about an equal period between the elections and the meeting of the conventions. This facility of action may have been due to the general sentiment in favor of the Constitution; or the rapidity of action may account for the slight development of the opposition.

In two commonwealths, Maryland and South Carolina, deliberation and delays in the election and the assembling of the conventions resulted in an undoubted majority in favor of the new instrument; but for the latter state the popular vote has never been figured out.

In one of the states, Pennsylvania, the proceedings connected with the ratification of the Constitution were conducted with unseemly haste.

In the adoption of the Constitution, says James Wilson, we have the gratifying spectacle of "a whole people exercising its first and greatest power—performing an act of sovereignty original and unlimited." Without questioning the statement that for juristic purposes the Constitution may be viewed as an expression of the will of the whole people, a historical view of the matter requires an analysis of "the people" into its constituent elements. In other words, how many of "the people" favored the adoption of the Constitution, and how many opposed it?

At the very outset, it is necessary to recall that the question whether a constitutional Convention should be held was not submitted to popular vote, and that it was not specially passed upon by the electors in chosing the members of the legislatures which selected the delegates.

In the second place, the Constitution was not submitted to popular ratification. The referendum was not unknown at that time, but it was not a fixed principle of American politics. At all events, such a procedure does not seem to have crossed the minds of the members of the Convention, and long afterward, Marshall stated that ratification by state conventions was the only mode conceivable. In view of the fact that there was no direct popular vote taken on the Constitution, it is therefore impossible to ascertain the exact number of "the people" who favored its adoption.

The voters, who took part in the selection of delegates to the ratifying conventions in the states, may be considered as having been divided into four elements: those who were consciously in favor of the Constitution, those who were just as consciously against it, those who were willing to leave the matter to the discretion of their elected representatives, and those who voted blindly.

The proportions which these four groups bear to one another cannot be determined, but certain facts may be brought out which will throw light on the great question: How many of the people favored the adoption of the Constitution?

The first fact to be noted in this examination is that a considerable proportion of the adult white male population was debarred from participating in the elections of delegates to the ratifying state conventions by the prevailing property qualifications on the suffrage. The determination of these suffrage qualifications was left to the state legislatures; and in general they adopted the property restrictions already imposed on voters for members of the lower branch of the state legislatures. . . .

At all events, the disfranchisement of the masses through property qualifications and ignorance and apathy contributed largely to the facility with which the personalty-interest representatives carried the day. The latter were alert everywhere, for they knew, not as a matter of theory, but as a practical matter of dollars and cents, the value of the new Constitution. They were well informed. They were conscious of the identity of their interests. They were well organized. They knew for weeks in advance, even before the Constitution was sent to the states for ratification, what the real nature of the contest was. They resided for the most part in the towns, or the more thickly populated areas, and they could marshall their forces quickly and effectively. They had also the advantage of appealing to all discontented persons who exist in large numbers in every society and are ever anxious for betterment through some change in political machinery.

Talent, wealth, and professional abilities were, generally speaking, on the side of the Constitutionalists. The money to be spent in the campaign of education was on their side also; and it was spent in considerable sums for pamphleteering, organizing parades and demonstrations, and engaging the interest of the press. A small percentage of the enormous gain to come through the appreciation of securities alone would have financed no mean campaign for those days.

The opposition on the other hand suffered from the difficulties connected with getting a backwoods vote out to the town and county elections. This involved sometimes long journeys in bad weather, for it will be remembered that the elections were held in the late fall and winter. There were no such immediate personal gains to be made through the defeat of the Constitution, as were to be made by the security holders on the other side. It was true the debtors knew that they would probably have to settle their accounts in full and the small farmers were aware that taxes would have to be paid to discharge the national debt if the Constitution was adopted; and the debtors everywhere waged war against the Constitution—of this there is plenty of evidence. But they had no money to carry on their campaign; they were poor and uninfluential—the strongest battalions were not on their side. The wonder is that they came so near defeating the Constitution at the polls. . . .

CONCLUSIONS

At the close of this long and arid survey—partaking of the nature of catalogue—it seems worth while to bring together the important conclusions for political science which the data presented appear to warrant.

The movement for the Constitution of the United States was originated and carried through principally by four groups of personalty interests which had been adversely affected under the Articles of Confederation: money, public securities, manufactures, and trade and shipping.

The first firm steps toward the formation of the Constitution were taken by a small and active group of men immediately interested through their personal possessions in the outcome of their labors.

No popular vote was taken directly or indirectly on the proposition to call the Convention which drafted the Constitution.

A large propertyless mass was, under the prevailing suffrage qualifications, excluded at the outset from participation (through representatives) in the work of framing the Constitution.

The members of the Philadelphia Convention which drafted the Constitution were, with a few exceptions, immediately, directly, and personally interested in, and derived economic advantages from, the establishment of the new system.

The Constitution was essentially an economic document based upon the concept that the fundamental private rights of property are anterior to government and morally beyond the reach of popular majorities.

The major portion of the members of the Convention are on record as recognizing the claim of property to a special and defensive position in the Constitution.

In the ratification of the Constitution, about three-fourths of the adult males failed to vote on the question, having abstained from the elections at which delegates to the state conventions were chosen, either on account of their indifference or their disfranchisement by property qualifications.

The Constitution was ratified by a vote of probably not more than one-sixth of the adult males.

It is questionable whether a majority of the voters participating in the elections for the state conventions in New York, Massachusetts, New Hampshire, Virginia, and South Carolina, actually approved the ratification of the Constitution.

The leaders who supported the Constitution in the ratifying conventions represented the same economic groups as the members of the Philadelphia Convention; and in a large number of instances they were also directly and personally interested in the outcome of their efforts.

In the ratification, it became manifest that the line of cleavage for and against the Constitution was between substantial personalty interests on the one hand and the small farming and debtor interests on the other.

The Constitution was not created by "the whole people" as the jurists have said; neither was it created by "the states" as Southern nullifiers long contended; but it was the work of a consolidated group whose interests knew no state boundaries and were truly national in their scope.

THE CONSTITUTION AS
A CONFLICT OF IDEAS

12 FROM *Cecilia Kenyon*
An Economic Interpretation of the
Constitution After Fifty Years

I

It is now a half-century since the publication in 1913 of Charles A. Beard's *An Economic Interpretation of the Constitution.* Rarely has a single book had so great an influence upon the writing and teaching of American history, or waited so long for sustained and comprehensive evaluation. By 1936 its thesis was found to be dominant in textbooks prepared for college use, and a few years later it was near the top of a list of books judged most influential by a group of leaders in various intellectual disciplines. Few would dispute its central role in shaping the image of America during this period, but many scholars today would question its validity. Within the last decade the book and its thesis have been subjected to severe criticism. It is perhaps premature to conclude that Beard's interpretation has been demolished, but it seems certain that it will never again attain its former supremacy. For although the recent attacks may not have disproved

SOURCE: Cecilia Kenyon, " 'An Economic Interpretation of the Constitution After Fifty Years," in *Centennial Review,* VII, No. 3 (Summer 1963), pp. 327–345. Reprinted by permission of the publisher and the author.

Beard's thesis, they have exposed the insufficiency of his evidence and raised serious questions about the validity of his reasoning. Thus the book and its reception present a strange chapter in American intellectual history. The immediate reaction to its publication was mixed. As might be expected, the argument that the primary motivation of the authors and advocates of the Constitution was the desire to further their class and personal economic interests seemed outrageous to those accustomed to regarding the Founding Fathers as patriots if not heroes. There was also, in that early period before the first world war, a certain amount of careful, scholarly criticism. But within a generation, the bulk of the articulate scholarly community seemed to have accepted *An Economic Interpretation* as the proper view of the Constitution. One might say that *the* economic interpretation was solidly established in American historiography. It remained so until the mid-fifties. It was then savagely attacked and is now, apparently, very much on the defensive. These circumstances provoke a number of interesting questions. Why was the book, now believed by many to be a thoroughly bad piece of scholarship, so long accepted so uncritically by so many serious and able students of American history? Why did a concerted and multi-prolonged attack not get underway for nearly half a century? Was there some form of cultural determinism at work which first compelled a widespread acceptance, and later shifted to a widespread rejection, of Beard? Was there, indeed, an element of economic determinism involved which influenced not only those who accepted, but also (ironically) those who now consciously reject a general theory of economic determinism? No final answer can be given to questions such as these, for they belong in the realm of the speculative. It is nevertheless tempting, and perhaps fruitful, to explore them. Before this can be done, it is necessary first to examine the thesis set forth in *An Economic Interpretation of the Constitution.*

II

The ambiguities in Beard's thesis have been recognized for many years by adherents and critics alike. The most important of these, because it is absolutely central to his argument, is the question of precisely what Beard meant by the terms *economic inter-pretation* and *economic determinism*. Beard chose the former of these as the title for his book, but he used both terms in the course of developing his thesis, and it therefore becomes important to determine what meaning he gave to each, and particularly, whether he distinguished between the two. It is my belief that he never defined either term with precision and that he used them more or less interchangeably. In the first chapter, "Historical Interpretation in the United States," Beard used *economic interpretation* six times (plus once in a footnote) and *economic determinism* four times   Although this is the chapter which introduces the new interpretation and at the same time justifies its application, there is no systematic, comprehensive definition of it. Beard refers to ". . . the hypothesis that economic elements are the chief factors in the development of political institutions" (p. 6), and in the same paragraph states that: "The theory of economic determinism has not been tried out in American history, and until it is tried out, it cannot be found wanting" (p. 7). The implication would seem to be that it is this theory which is to be "tried out" in the following chapter. A few pages later, Beard states that ". . . the inquiry which follows is based upon the political science of James Madison" (p. 14), which is then characterized as ". . . a masterly statement of the theory of economic determinism in politics" (p. 15). He then turns to a summary of the ". . . requirements for an economic interpretation of the formation and adoption of the Constituton . . ." (p. 16). These requirements seem to boil down to a positive correlation statistically between different sets of economic interests and their respective positions for or against the Constitution. If substantially all of one group of interests supported the Constitution and substantially all of the other opposed it, Beard suggests, one may conclude that ". . . the direct, compelling motive in both cases was the economic advantages which the beneficiaries expected would accrue to themselves first, from their actions" pp. 17-18).

From these statements in the introductory chapter, we may conclude, first, that Beard did not distinguish between *economic determinism* and *economic interpretation*. Certainly there is no clear, explicit differentiation between the two, and the terms seem to be used as if they were synonymous. One may conclude, secondly, that Beard's conception of the proper use of statistical method is a rather crude one. Even if one discovered a perfect correlation between the factors he suggests, one would not be justified in inferring an exclusive, causal relationship between simple economic interest and the position taken on the Constitution, without exploring other factors which might be relevant. The methodological fallacy in such an inference is easily illustrated by the story of the beginning student in sociology who discovered that rural Sweden had a substantially larger stork population than urban Sweden, that the human birth rate in rural Sweden was correspondingly higher than in urban Sweden, and who accordingly concluded from this demonstrable correlation, that storks were indeed responsible for the delivery of Swedish infants. The point is obvious: one cannot automatically exclude all other evidence as irrelevant and immaterial simply because one finds a statistical correlation of the sort Beard thought he had established.

Thus a sophisticated social scientist today would, I think, regard Beard's introduction with raised eyebrows and approach the body of the book in a skeptical frame of mind. In spite of the ambiguity and crudity apparent in this first chapter, however, Beard's main point was made quite clearly: economic factors were the decisive element in determining one's attitude toward the constitution of 1787.

A second major element in his general thesis, first presented in these early pages and then elaborated on throughout the book, appears to be equally clear at first glance. Beard saw the economic situation of the time as one in which men could be placed in one of the two categories of interest groups with relative ease and certainty. On the one hand belonged ". . . the merchants, money lenders, security holders, manufacturers, shippers, capitalists, and financiers and their professional associates," and on the other, ". . . the non-slave-holding farmers and the debtors" (p. 17). The former group are subsequently referred to as those whose property was in personalty, the latter, the agrarians, or those whose property was in realty or land. A careful reading of the text, and a thoughtful consideration of the economic division as Beard pursues them in the course of his work, ought to have given the critical scholar some doubts. Where, for example, should the slave-holding farmers and planters be placed? Their slaves were personal property, but their land was real property. It is significant that they are not mentioned in the above classification. Or what about the designation of a debtor class *per se?* Were there no debtors among those whose interests were in personalty? If being in debt was an important factor in the economic situation of 1787-1788, then surely Beard should have explored it carefully. He did not.

A third factor in *An Economic Interpretation* is equally vulnerable on methodological grounds and has probably been the most consistently criticized part of the book since its publication. This is Beard's ambiguity with respect to the question whether the authors and leading advocates of the Constitution were motivated by the desire for personal and immediate economic gain. Were they, as the saying goes, simply out to line their own pocketbooks? Beard's handling of this question is very curious. Let it be said, first, that he explicitly denied making any such charge. "The purpose of such an inquiry [into the economic interests of the members of the Philadelphia Convention] is not, of course, to show that the Constitution was made for the personal benefit of the members of the Convention. Far from it." The point, rather, was whether they represented ". . . distinct groups whose economic interests they understood and felt in concrete, definite form through their own personal experience with identical property rights . . ." (p. 73). Why make such a distinction? Did Beard feel some compunction about accusing the Founding Fathers of very personal self-interest? Did he think it less obnoxious to charge them with shared, group self-interest rather than with individual self-interest? Or did he think it somehow more scientific to work in terms of group interests rather than personal interests? I suspect that both considerations were present. What seems more certain, however, is that Beard never quite made up his mind about what he thought, and that on both the ethical and the scientific points he remained muddled, confusing and confused.

An example of ambiguity on this particular point is to be found in his treatment of the significance of holding large or small amounts of the public securities which might be redeemed if a strong central government were instituted, and which therefore afforded a motive for security holders to support the Constitution. One of the delegates to the Convention, George Mason of Virginia, a very wealthy planter, was reported by Mason's biographer to have had extensive holdings in land for apparently speculative purposes, to have been interested in promoting manufactures in Virginia, to have held some fifty thousand dollars in personal property besides his slaves, and to have been a creditor to the extent of thirty thousand dollars without owing anything himself. After taking this information from Mason's biographer, Beard adds that Mason apparently had very little of his personal wealth in public securities. The Treasury records showed ". . . one small entry of a few hundred dollars worth of threes and sixes" (p. 128). Now, although Mason was, during part of the Convention, an enthusiastic supporter of a strong central government, in the end he refused to sign the Constitution and campaigned vigorously against it in Virginia. Because of the diversity and extent of his property, Mason would seem to be difficult to fit into the thesis on a number of counts, but the point I want to make at the moment is the relative smallness of his holdings in public securities. In a later chapter, Beard makes this statement: "The point, it may be repeated, is not the amount but the practical information derived from holding even one certificate of the nominal value of $10" (Footnote, p. 272). Yet, several pages later, Beard says, "Inasmuch as so many leaders in the movement for ratification were large security holders, and inasmuch as securities constituted such a large proportion of personalty, this economic interest must have formed a very considerable dynamic element, if not the preponderating element, in bringing about the adoption of the new system" (p. 290). If we put the facts about Mason together with these two statements, the lack of rigorousness in Beard's interpretation should become clear. If a single $10 certificate were enough to incline one toward the Constitution, then Mason should logically have been so inclined. Yet the last statement quoted seems to emphasize the *large amount* of security holdings, and the *large proportion* of such holdings to other personal property. Accordingly, Mason should not have been among the ". . . dynamic element in bringing about the adoption of the new system." And in fact he was not. These two positions taken by

Beard, one that the amount was not significant, the other that it was, do not seem to be entirely consistent. If the statement about the $10 certificate had been made in reference to the members of the Convention, the two attitudes could be more easily reconciled. Both, however, were expressed in the context of the ratification controversy. I think they reflect the lack of clarity and consistency in Beard's own thought with respect to the motivation of those who participated in the process of framing and adopting the Constitution.

Even more remarkable is the treatment of Alexander Hamilton and James Madison, especially of Hamilton. Both were extremely important in the movement for a new Constitution but neither, according to Beard, was very wealthy. Furthermore, Madison apparently owned no public securities at all (p. 125), and Hamilton no more than a "petty amount." Their motivation, then, was apparently not primarily economic. In fact, Beard devotes about ten pages to a demonstration that Hamilton was *not* so motivated, either in 1787-1788 or during his term as Secretary of the Treasury, and he concludes: ". . . an extensive augmentation of his personal fortune was no consideration with him. The fact that he died a poor man is conclusive evidence of this fact. That he was swayed throughout the period of the formation of the Constitution by large policies of government—not by any of the personal interests so often ascribed to him—must therefore be admitted" (p. 114). Beard does not make a similarly explicit assertion about Madison's motivation, but seems to suggest that Madison was a politically oriented man. "His inclinations were all toward politics. . . ." And "The postponement of his marriage until 1794 enabled him to devote himself to political pursuits rather than commercial or economic interests of any kind" (p. 125). The fact that neither man fits into the general thesis of economic determinism, or interpretation, does not, as Beard rightly points out, vitiate that thesis. Still, it is a little odd that these two, who are such active and effective leaders among the "dynamic element" responsible for the Constitution, were not apparently influenced by economic considerations. If Madison and Hamilton, why not others? If economic considerations were irrelevant in their cases, could the same not be said of others, including others who did own personal property which might have been beneficially affected by the proposed new government? It is here that I would emphasize a point made earlier in this essay: a simple statistical correlation between two factors does not necessarily establish a causal relationship between them in the presence of other possible causal factors. In his treatment of Hamilton and Madison, Beard does admit the existence of another such factor. He admits political man—perhaps even patriotic man—into the picture. This is important from the methodological point of view.

Less important, but still intriguing, is the ethical consideration. Why did Beard take so much pains to clear Alexander Hamilton of what he referred to as "improper motives?" If Beard really believed in a theory of economic determinism, he presumably believed that men's economic interests *determined* their behavior, in which case, economically self-interested behavior would be not only natural but inevitable, and therefore logically not "improper." Even if Beard believed only in a less rigid economic interpretation—*i.e.*, that economic interests were very likely to influence men's behavior—such economically motivated behavior would seem to be quite normal and natural and therefore not particularly culpable. Why, then, does Beard single Hamilton out for this extraordinary clean bill of health?

There is yet another curious aspect to this treatment of Hamilton. Hamilton is presented as the great organizing genius who made of the new Constitution "... a real instrument bottomed on all the substantial interests of the time" (p. 100). He did this by perceiving what groups "... would have to be rallied to the new government," and he accomplished the job of rallying them by organization and consolidation. "Without the conciliation and positive support of these powerful elements in American society, the new government could not have been founded or continued. With keen insight, Hamilton saw this" (pp. 100-102). These interests were, of course, those of substantial wealth and especially personal wealth. They were not those of "... small farmers and debtors and laboring mechanics. ..." (p. 103). Hamilton did not appeal to these latter. *"The road to power and glory did not yet lie in championing their cause"* (p. 103. Italics added).

Thus enter the hero; thus exit the theory of economic determinism? The picture of the framing, ratification, and institution of the new Constitution and government here given emphasizes the genius of a single individual, not himself motivated by economic interests, but using them in order to create a new political order and thus win power and glory. It is an admirable portrait of Hamilton, but it would appear to leave the concept of economic determinism in a somewhat dishevelled condition. It is still possible to emphasize the importance of economic factors, but they would now seem to have a serious rival for the role of dynamic forces. Beard presents them in these pages as if they were acted upon, not as if they were the prime stimuli to action. A sophisticated theory of economic determinism might be devised to take a Hamilton or two into account. It could be argued, for example, that the existing economic structure and its resultant social relations were bound to throw up a figure like Hamilton, a man born outside the pale of the privileged class, enormously talented, enormously ambitious, and inevitably compelled to identify himself with that class in order to fulfill himself. But this is not Beard's theory. He seems rather consistently to think in terms of conscious economic motivation, of deliberate and rational efforts on the part of men to satisfy their economic interests by political action. And his treatment of Hamilton makes it perfectly clear that he believes men *can choose not* to do so, for Hamilton did not advance his interests through political means, even though he could have. Some men, at least, are free agents. Again we may ask, if Hamilton, why not others among his colleagues? I would suggest, therefore, that Beard had no clearly worked-out theory of economic determinism or even of economic interpretation.

As one proceeds further into an examination of his thesis, one meets additional evidence of lack of clarity, sophistication, and consistency. Beard's simple view seemed to be that the substantial and especially the personal property interest groups in the country were adversely affected by conditions existing under the weak government established by the Articles of Confederation; that they united in order to institute a stronger central government which would both protect and foster their economic interests; that they wrote a Constitution deliberately designed for the purpose; and that the whole process of initiating, framing, and ratifying the Constitution was accomplished by the use of undemocratic methods.

I should like to turn now to the last two of these propositions. In the chapter entitled "The Constitution as an Economic Document," Beard summarizes the efforts of its authors under two headings:

"I. A government endowed with certain positive powers, but so constructed as to break the force of majority rule and vent invasions of the property rights of minorities.

II. Restrictions on the state legislatures which had been so vigorous in their attacks on capital" (p. 154).

Let it be said at once that on the second of these propositions, Beard was correct. The Founding Fathers did want to prevent state governments from enacting certain types of legislation injurious to the rights of property, and they wrote into the Constitution specific and explicit provisions to effect their purpose. These are to be found in Article I, Section 10. Let it also be said, however, that the Founding Fathers did not prohibit these kinds of laws to the national legislature. It is not unreasonable to infer that a corresponding aim was the establishment of a national economic system to replace one fragmented by the diverse laws of thirteen—and eventually more—separate states.

With respect to the first of the two propositions, Beard is on more dubious ground. The structure of the central government to which Beard refers was, of course, the system of separation of powers and checks and balances. It is perfectly true that the authors of the Constitution did create such a structure. It is also true that this system was explained and elaborated on in *The Federalist Papers,* from which Beard quotes. And it is true that the Founding Fathers had some doubts that the will of the majority would always be wise, or right, or just. But it is also true that those who opposed the Constitution had these same doubts, that they especially feared the legislative majority of a national government, and that they criticized the Constitution on the grounds that it violated the principle of separation of powers, and that it did not have enough checks and balances. Beard did not report these Anti-Federalist ideas, and apparently either did not notice them, or did not see the significance they had for his theory. Consider first the logic of the situation. If the authors and advocates of the Constitution wanted to transfer certain powers over the economy from the state governments to the central government, the implication would seem to be that they trusted the latter more than the former. They may have been fearful of certain types of majority decisions, but they did establish a national government committed to the fundamental principle of majority rule, subject to a qualified executive and potentially to judicial review. They presumably believed that their interests would be safer with a majority in the national legislature than with those in the separate state legislatures. Indeed, Beard himself makes this point more or less explicitly: "The economic corollary of this system [of separation of powers and checks and balances] is as follows: Property interests may, through their superior weight in power and intelligence, secure advantageous legislation whenever necessary, and they may, at the same time obtain immunity from control by parliamentary majorities" (p. 161). Leaving aside for the moment the interesting question of how all this is to be done, it is clear that Beard thought the Founding Fathers thought they would have, or could control, a majority in the national legislature. If so, would it not then be logical for their opponents to be fearful of such a majority? The fact is that the Anti-Federalists did distrust the national legislative majority, and dwelt fervently on the necessity of restraining and checking it. Beard's infatuation with his thesis of economic determinism blinded him not only to the expressed views of the opponents of the Constitution, but to the logic of the situation and to the actual facts of politics.

Earlier in the book he had referred to the antagonism between the debtor and creditor classes, and to "its institutional reflex in the Constitution" (p. 32). The system of separation of powers and checks and balances was interpreted by him to be a part of that "institutional reflex." But was it? Both sides wanted it, the Anti-Federalists wanting a bit more of it. Were the "reflexes" of one group inappropriate to the accomplishment of its aims? Or were both sets of "reflexes" properly geared to achieve the results desired by each of the opposing groups? To ask this question is to reveal the weakness of Beard's theory as a tool for political analysis. It would seem that the mills of economic determinism grind either rather coarsely, or rather erratically. They do not, or at least did not in this instance, produce separate political ideas for different and allegedly conflicting economic interests. Consideration of these questions also suggests a very peculiar aspect of Beard's interpretation. That is his assumption of extraordinary rationality in the political behavior of men. With remarkable consistency, Beard assumes that men, at least his men, will not only see their interests clearly, but will also see precisely how to go about securing them. It is a strange position for a man of the twentieth century to take, and very strange indeed for one who claimed to have adopted the political science of James Madison as the foundation for his own work.

There remains to be discussed the final part of the thesis, the argument that the Constitution was framed and adopted in an undemocratic way by the use of undemocratic methods, and that it almost certainly did not have the support of the majority of all free, adult males. It is interesting and sometimes exasperating to follow Beard's reasoning as he develops this theme throughout the book. He twists back and forth from one position to another on some issues, just as he shifts back and forth from a position of self-conscious realism to one of unconscious idealism.

One aspect of the subject that gave Beard a great deal of trouble was the suffrage, especially, the property qualifications for voting and their effect on the size of the electorate. He was confronted with two separate problems. The first was one of fact: approximately what proportion of the free adult male population was excluded by the qualifications existing in the various states? The data he had to go on were not very precise or comprehensive, and he can perhaps not be blamed for that. Unfortunately, however, he was not consistent in his interpretation and use of the information which he did have. In the early pages of the book, for example, he refers to "the mass of men" and "a great number of adult males" who were legally excluded from the suffrage (p. 34). Later this has become "large portion," and he also states that ". . . the wide distribution of real property created an extensive electorate and in most rural regions gave the legislatures a broad popular basis" (p. 71). Elsewhere he suggests that probably ". . . nowhere were more than one-third of the adult males disfranchised by the property qualification," and in some places perhaps fewer (p. 242). These statements are not flatly contradictory, but there is enough difference in tone between the first and the second to convey very different impressions as to how democratic the suffrage was in actual practice. It is significant, I think, that the context of the first was Beard's introduction of the undemocratic character of the constitution-making process, while that of the second was a statement to the effect that the existing property qualifications alone were not a sufficient safeguard for the interests of personal property.

These different contexts point up the second problem Beard had in relating the suffrage to the allegedly undemocratic character of the Constitution and of the process by which it was made and adopted. Perhaps it would be more accurate to refer to the problem as one which Beard had, but of which he was not sufficiently aware. For he was handling two political universes in *An Economic Interpretation*. One was that of the whole free adult male population; the other was that of the legally qualified electorate. Most of the action in his drama takes place in this second world, where the lines are drawn between the two major interest groups—the agrarian and debtors, and the capitalists and creditors, both of which consist of men of property.

Now, if the Constitution was itself undemocratic, or was undemocratically framed and ratified according to the criterion of the suffrage, then the agrarian-debtor class must share in the responsibility, for the suffrage qualifications provided for in the Constitution and also used in the process of establishing it, were those then existing in the separate states. For all but one state, then, the two groups were both undemocratic, when judged on this one point It would seem to be somewhat gratuitous and inappropriate to emphasize this fact for only one of the groups. A more important question is that of both context and criterion. It would seem to be obvious that the prevailing practice and consensus of the period was in favor of property qualifications for voting. What, then, is the point of making so much of a factor that was not at issue in the contemporary controversy? Of course, a restricted suffrage is undemocratic by twentieth century standards, and clearly, the separation of powers and checks and balances was undemocratic by Beard's own personal standards. But *neither* of these two principles was challenged by any substantial portion of either side in the controversy of 1787-1788. If so, then what were the criteria for democracy in that period, and what criteria should a modern scholar use in attempting an analysis of its institutions? These are questions which Beard did not consider. Indeed, he seemed completely unaware of them or of their importance for systematic political analysis.

Although we may question the analytical propriety of mixing the two political worlds as he has, we may easily agree with Beard that the exclusion of propertyless men from participating in the formation and ratification of the Constitution did render that process undemocratic. Beard's contention that the process within the world of the legally enfranchised was also undemocratic is less readily apparent. His case does not include charges of widespread fraud, corruption, or intimidation, though he does suggest that the ratifying conventions were held with undue haste in some of the states. It is difficult, really, to pin down precisely what he thought was undemocratic in the methods of the eventually victorious party.

One element in the process which disturbed him was the irregular scheme devised by the leaders of the movement to secure their goals after having failed in their efforts to amend the Articles of Confederation by the regular and legal methods. This method had required the unanimous consent of all thirteen states, and it had proved impossible to secure this. Beard uses such phrases as "ostensibly" and "outward signs of regularity" (pp. 63, 64), to suggest the conspiratorial nature of the early plans for calling a constitutional convention.

After the leaders had succeeded in this endeavor, they proceeded to make sure that the delegates chosen by the state legislatures were advocates of their point of view. In this, they were "... favored by the inertness, ignorance, and indifference of the masses, and the confidence of the legislatures in their ability to exercise the ultimate control through the ratifying power" (p. 64). Of the next state in the process, the Convention and the actual framing of the Constitution, Beard has very little to say. One chapter, "The Political Doctrines of the Members of the Convention," contains a highly selective collection of disparate ideas, but there is no sustained study of the way in which the men at Philadelphia worked through the various proposals, ironed out the differences, and finally produced a document which may indeed have been beneficial to the immediate economic interests of their class, but which was also to serve as the fundamental law for a united people for nearly one hundred and seventy-five years—and perhaps longer. Indeed, the most remarkable feature of *An Economic Interpretation* is its omission of any serious consideration of the actual work of the Convention. If the importance of that work is accurately gauged by the random and casual attention given to it by Beard, one wonders just what those men were doing throughout the nearly four months they spent in Philadelphia in the summer of 1787.

Superior organization, intelligence, and effort seem to be the main ingredients in Beard's contention that the Constitution was put over by undemocratic means, though he gives some weight also to iniquities of representation in some of the states, as well as to the haste with which a few of the Conventions were held. Some weight should certainly be given to these two latter factors, but much of Beard's argumentation on the question seems open to question.

The idea that the proponents of the Constitution were well organized, active, alert, and able politicians runs throughout *An Economic Interpretation*. That their opposition was not, is also expressed. Beard speaks of the difficulties of getting out the vote in rural districts where the polling places might be a considerable distance away from an elector's home, and of the lack of money for campaign expenditures on the part of the debtors (p. 252). After discussing the probable proportion of adult males legally unqualified to vote, Beard says: "Far more were disfranchised through apathy and lack of understanding of the significance of politics. It is a noteworthy fact that only a small proportion of the population entitled to vote took the trouble to go to the polls until the hot political contests of the Jeffersonian era" (p. 242). And again: "At all events, the disfranchisement of the masses through property qualifications and ignorance and apathy contributed largely to the facility with which the personalty-interest representatives carried the day" (p. 251).

In recounting the process of ratification in the Massachusetts Convention, Beard accepts the opinion of an earlier historian that had a vote been taken when the Convention first opened, the Constitution would probably have been rejected. It was eventually accepted by a vote of 187-168, and Beard states: "One can scarcely escape the conclusion that the victory in eloquence, logic, and pure argumentation lay on the side of the Federalists. . . ." (p. 227). Apart from the implications for a theory of economic determinism of such a conclusion, one may ask, was it undemocratic that these factors should influence the Massachusetts Convention? Would Beard exclude logic, eloquence, and argumentation from democratic politics?

The discussion of ratification in both its electoral and convention phases reflects an oddly unrealistic and unhistoric conception of policies during the period, and in general. For one thing, it is absurd to speak of eligible voters being disfranchised through "apathy" and "lack of understanding of the significance of politics." This notion might have some validity if applied to a newly or temporarily franchised group, such as existed in New York state for this particular election. But the remainder of the electorate was of relatively long standing. Its members had had years, if not the heritage of generations, to learn the significance of politics. If it remained apathetic during the contest, that was its responsibility—and, we might add, its right.

The second comment that can be made about this part of Beard's analysis is that the conditions and factors he notes were not peculiar to the ratification elections and conventions alone. The physical and institutional situation which made it difficult to get out the backwoods or rural vote was the same as it had been in the few years previous to 1787-1788, when some of the state legislatures enacted their laws for the relief of debtors. Was "apathy," "lack of understanding of the significance of politics," and inferior organization on the part of the personalty-interest groups responsible for the successful enactment of these laws? If so, were these laws put into effect by "undemocratic" means? It seems to me that Beard never really succeeds in explaining how and why the groups which had been unable to prevent the enactment of laws injurious to their interests in the arena of post-Revolution state politics, were, nevertheless, able to swing enough votes, either in the electoral or the convention stage of the campaign, to secure adoption of a whole new government which was, according to Beard, designed to protect and promote those interests. To a modern political scientist, the probable hypothetical factor to search for would be the swing or marginal vote, that is to say, a segment of the electorate not rigidly committed to either of two large and competing political groups. Beard does touch on this vote when discussing the apparent shifts in the New Hampshire, Massachusetts, and New York ratifying conventions. But it seems to disturb him because it is difficult to explain in terms of his theory of economic determinism or interpretation. What he does not seem to contemplate is the possible role of such a vote in the electoral stage as well.

This omission, I think, is symptomatic of the Beard thesis and has had until recently, an unfortunate effect on the historiographical image of the period. The tendency has been to see two more or less permanent groupings or parties from the pre-Revolutionary debate on, and to make too little allowance for the marginal or independent voter, or for precisely that apathetic and indifferent element Beard mentioned. His failure to explore these elements more carefully is regrettable, but was a logical consequence of his intellectual frame of reference. This was dichotomous. In the introductory chapter Beard referred to "economic groups or classes" as a causal factor in relation to the formation of the Constitution as opposed to "abstract causes remote from the chief business of life—gaining a livelihood" (p. 17). Later he states the fundamental question to be considered: "Did they [the delegates to the Philadelphia Convention] represent distinct groups whose economic interests they understood and felt in concrete, definite form through their own personal experience with identical property rights, or were they working merely under the guidance of abstract principles of political science?" (p. 73). This question is eventually answered: "But enough has been said to show that the concept of the Constitution as a piece of abstract legislation reflecting no group interests and recognizing no economic antagonisms is entirely false" (p. 188). In these three statements, Beard draws a sharp opposition between economic interests on the one hand, and abstract principles on the other. The implication is clearly that political reality and political realism are made up of the former. But is not this "realistic" conception of politics a bit unrealistic? It is very narrow, and it is very exclusive. There is so much that it seems to leave out, so much for which it seems to provide no adequate information. For example, it may possibly explain why George Washington supported the Constitution, but does it explain why this very support was, or at the time was believed to be, an important factor in getting others to support it? Or does it explain why he was so overwhelmingly elected as the first President? Does it explain how or why the authors of the Constitution put into it a prohibition against any religious tests for holding office? Or why this provision was bitterly crticized? Does it explain why, as Beard himself concludes, Alexander Hamilton was *not* influenced by economic considerations? It is not necessary, in order to consider economic factors in politics, to exclude all others. Nor is it necessary, in order to be realistic, to exclude abstract ideas. It is possible that abstract ideas, or just plain ideas, play a role in politics. Certainly Beard presented no evidence in *An Economic Interpretation* to prove that they played no role in the great events of 1787-1788. For all its alleged realism, the book presents a narrowly unrealistic picture of a very rich and complex subject....

PART FIVE

Ratification: A Conflict of Ideas

There is no simple explanation for the origins of the Federal Constitution or why ratification divided the country so sharply. Citizens did calculate how a change in government might affect their material interests, though there was much less unity among classes than Beard thought. Urban groups, especially speculators, merchants, artisans, and shopkeepers generally favored a strong central government, but most Americans were farmers, and the rural regions were split. States that had fared poorly under the Confederation were more willing to make a change. Thus Georgia looked to a strong national government to remove the Indians who blocked its development and New Jersey hoped to escape paying taxes on imports purchased through New York City which enriched the treasury of its neighbor On the other hand, many state officials feared a loss of power and influence if there was a strong national government.

Regardless of how one accounts for the motives of the supporters and opponents of the Constitution, the ratification debates revealed profound differences in political thinking. The anti-Consitutionalists were traditionalists who measured the proposed Constitution against the conventional political wisdom of revolutionary America and discovered radical and dangerous departures. The pro-Constitutionalists shared their opponents' fear of tyranny but believed that innovations were necessary. Dissatisfaction with the Confederation led some to think freshly about how to preserve liberty in a large and diverse republic that they thought could neither prosper nor survive without strong central government.

THE DILEMMA OF
REPUBLICAN GOVERNMENT

*Both sides in the ratification debates believed that powerful forces en-
dangered the success of the republican experiment. Men by nature
were aggressive and ambitious, jealous of their neighbors and easily
corrupted by the lure of power to advance their own interests at the
expense of others. The revolutionary generation believed, however, that
appropriate political arrangements could tame faction, enable conflicting interests to secure justice, and lay the foundation of a republic
that was peaceful, strong, and free. In the following selections, anti-
Constitutionalists express widespread fear that the new Constitution
would deliver the country into the hands of aristocrats. Supporters of
the Constitution vigorously denied that it was a plot of the rich and
well born. Nowhere in American political thought have the dangers to
liberty been analyzed more subtly, shrewdly, and realistically than in
Federalist No. 10 reprinted below, one of eighty-five essays Alexander
Hamilton, James Madison, and John Jay wrote to convince their
countrymen that the Constitution was "a republican remedy for the
disease most incident to republican government."*

ANTI-CONSTITUTIONALISTS

13 FROM *James Lincoln*
The South Carolina Convention

Hon. James Lincoln, of *Ninety-six*, declared, that if ever any
person rose in a public assembly with diffidence, he then did;
if ever any person felt himself deeply interested in what he

SOURCE: James Lincoln in Jonathan Elliott, Comp., *The Debates in the
Several State Conventions on the Adoption of the Federal Constitution as
Recommended by the General Convention at Phildelphia*, 2nd ed., **IV**, pp.
312–315 (Philadelphia: Lippincott, 1896).

thought a good cause, and at the same time lamented the want of abilities to support it, it was he. On a question on which gentlemen, whose abilities would do honor to the senate of ancient Rome, had enlarged with so much eloquence and learning, who could venture without anxiety and diffidence? He had not the vanity to oppose his opinion to such men; he had not the vanity to suppose he could place this business in any new light; but the justice he owed to his constituents—the justice he owed to his own feelings, which would perhaps upbraid him hereafter, if he indulged himself so far as to give merely a silent vote on this great question—impelled him, reluctantly impelled him, to intrude himself on the house. He had, for some years past, turned his thoughts towards the politics of this country; he long since perceived that not only the federal but the state Constitution required much the hand of correction and revision. They were both formed in times of confusion and distress, and it was a matter of wonder they were so free from defects as we found them. That they were imperfect, no one would deny; and that something must be done to remedy those imperfections, was also evident; but great care should be taken that, by endeavoring to do some good, we should not do an infinite deal of mischief. He had listened with eager attention to all the arguments in favor of the Constitution; but he solemnly declared that the more he heard, the more he was persuaded of its evil tendency. What does this proposed Constitution do? It changes, totally changes, the form of your present government. From a well-digested, well-formed democratic, you are at once rushing into an aristocratic government. What have you been contending for these ten years past? Liberty! What is liberty? The power of governing yourselves. If you adopt this Constitution, have you this power? No: you give it into the hands of a set of men who live one thousand miles distant from you. Let the people but once trust their liberties out of their own hands, and what will be the consequence? First, a haughty, imperious aristocracy; and ultimately, a tyrannical monarchy. No people on earth are, at this day, so free as the people of America. All other nations are, more or less, in a state of slavery. They owe their constitutions partly to chance, and partly to the sword; but that of America is the offspring of their choice—the darling of their bosom: and was there ever an instance in the world that a people in this situation, possessing all that Heaven could give on earth, all that human wisdom and valor could procure—was there ever a people so situated, as calmly and deliberately to convene themselves together for the express purpose of considering whether they should give away or retain those inestimable blessings? In the name of God, were we a parcel of children, who would cry and quarrel for a hobbyhorse, which, when we were once in possession of, we quarrel with and throw it away? It is said this Constitution is an experiment; but all regular-bred physicians are cautious of experiments. If the constitution be crazed a little, or somewhat feeble, is it therefore necessary to kill it in order to cure it? Surely not. There are many parts of this Constitution he objected to: some few of them had not been mentioned; he would therefore request some information thereon. The President holds his employment for four years; but he may hold it for fourteen times four years: in short, he may hold it so long that it will be impossible, without another revolution, to displace him. You do not put the same check on him that you do on your own state governor—a man born and bred among you; a man over whom you have a continual and watchful eye; a man who, from the very nature of his situation, it is almost impossible can do you any injury: this man, you say, shall not be elected for more than four years; and yet this mighty, this omnipotent governor-general may be elected for years and years.

He would be glad to know why, in this Constitution, there is a total silence with regard to the liberty of the press. Was it forgotten? Impossible! Then it must have been purposely omitted; and with what design, good or bad, he left the world to judge. The liberty of the press was the tyrant's scourge—it was the true friend and firmest supporter of civil liberty; therefore why pass it by in silence? He perceived that not till almost the very end of the Constitution was there any provision made for the nature or form of government we were to live under: he contended it should have been the very first article; it should have been, as it were, the groundwork or foundation on which it should have been built. But how is it? At the very end of the Constitution, there is a clause which says,—"The Congress of the United States shall guaranty to each state a republican form of government." But pray, who are the United States?—A President and four or five senators? Pray, sir, what security have we for a republican form of government, when it depends on the mere will and pleasure of a few men, who, with an army, navy, and rich treasury at their back, may change and alter it as they please? It may be said they will be sworn. Sir, the king of Great Britain, at his coronation, swore to govern his subjects with justice and mercy. We were then his subjects, and continued so for a long time after. He would be glad to know how he observed his oath. If, then, the king of Great Britain forswore himself, what security have we that a future President and four or five senators—men like himself—will think more solemnly of so sacred an obligation than he did?

Why was not this Constitution ushered in with the bill of rights? Are the people to have no rights? Perhaps this same President and Senate would, by and by, declare them. He much feared they would. He concluded by returning his hearty thanks to the gentleman who had so nobly opposed this Constitution: it was supporting the cause of the people; and if ever any one deserved the title of man of the people, he, on this occasion, most certainly did.

14 FROM *Patrick Dollard* *The South Carolina Convention*

Mr. President, I rise, with the greatest diffidence, to speak on this occasion, not only knowing myself unequal to the task, but believing this to be the most important question that ever the good people of this state were called together to deliberate upon. This Constitution has been ably supported, and ingeniously glossed over by many able and respectable gentlemen in this

SOURCE: Patrick Dollard in Jonathan Elliot, Comp., *The Debates in the Several State Conventions on the Adoption of the Federal Constitution as Recommended by the General Convention at Philadelphia,* 2nd ed., IV, pp. 336–338 (Philadelphia: Lippincott, 1896).

house, whose reasoning, aided by the most accurate eloquence, might strike conviction even in the predetermined breast, had they a good cause to support. Conscious that they have not, and also conscious of my inability to point out the consequences of its defects, which have in some measure been defined by able gentlemen in this house, I shall therefore confine myself within narrow bounds; that is, concisely to make known the sense and language of my constituents. The people of Prince Frederick's Parish, whom I have the honor to represent, are a brave, honest, and industrious people. In the late bloody contest, they bore a conspicuous part, when they fought, bled and conquered, in defence of their civil rights and privileges, which they expected to transmit untainted to their posterity. They are nearly all, to a man, opposed to this new Constitution, because, they say, they have omitted to insert a bill of rights therein, ascertaining and fundamentally establishing, the unalienable rights of men, without a full, free, and secure enjoyment of which there can be no liberty, and over which it is not necessary that a good government should have the control. They say that they are by no means against vesting Congress with ample and sufficient powers; but to make over to them, or any set of men, their birthright, comprised in Magna Charta, which this new Constitution absolutely does, they can never agree to. Notwithstanding this, they have the highest opinion of the virtues and abilities of the honorable gentlemen from this state, who represented us in the General Convention; and also a few other distinguished characters, whose names will be transmitted with honor to future ages; but I believe, at the same time, they are but mortal, and, therefore, liable to err; and as the virtue and abilities of those gentlemen will consequently recommend their being first employed in jointly conducting the reins of this government, they are led to believe it will commence in a moderate aristocracy: but, that it will, in its future operations, produce a monarchy, or a corrupt and oppressive aristocracy, they have no manner of doubt. Lust of dominion is natural in every soil, and the lover of power and superiority is as prevailing in the United States, at present, as in any part of the earth; yet in this country, depraved as it is, there still remains a strong regard for liberty: an American bosom is apt to glow at the sound of it, and the splendid merit of preserving that best gift of God, which is mostly expelled from every country in Europe, might stimulate Indolence, and animate even Luxury to consecrate herself at the altar of freedom.

My constituents are highly alarmed at the large and rapid strides which this new government has taken towards despotism. They say it is big with political mischiefs, and pregnant with a greater variety of impending woes to the good people of the Southern States, especially South Carolina, than all the plagues supposed to issue from the poisonous box of Pandora. They say it is particularly calculated for the meridian of despotic aristocracy; that it evidently tends to promote the ambitious views of a few able and designing men, and enslave the rest; that it carries with it the appearance of an old phrase, formerly made use of in despotic reigns, and especially by Archbishop Laud, in the reign of Charles I., that is, "non-resistance." They say they will resist against it; that they will not accept of it unless compelled by force of arms, which this new Constitution plainly threatens; and then, they say, your standing army, like Turkish janizaries enforcing despotic laws, must ram it down their throats with the points of bayonets. They warn the gentlemen of this Convention, as the guardians of their liberty, to beware how they will be accessory to the disposal of, or rather sacrificing, their dear-bought rights and privileges. This is the sense and language, Mr. President, of the people; and it is an old saying, and I believe a very true one, that the general voice of the people is the voice of God. The general voice of the people, to whom I am responsible, is against it. I shall never betray the trust reposed in me by them; therefore, shall give my hearty dissent.

PRO-CONSTITUTIONALISTS

15 FROM   *Edmund Pendleton*
            The Virginia Convention

. . . I am unfortunate enough to differ from the worthy member [Patrick Henry] in another circumstance He professes himself an advocate for the middling and lower classes of men. I profess to be a friend to the equal liberty of all men, from the palace to the cottage, without any other distinction than that between good and bad men. I appeal to my public life and private behavior, to decide whether I have departed from this rule. Since distinctions have been brought forth and communicated to the audience, and will be therefore disseminated, I beg gentlemen to take with them this observation—that distinctions have been produced by the opposition. From the friends of the new government they have heard none. None such are to be found in the organization of the paper before you.

Why bring into the debate the whims of writers—introducing the distinction of *well-born* from others? I consider every man *well-born* who comes into the world with an intelligent mind, and with all his parts perfect. I am an advocate for fixing our government on true republican principles, giving to the poor man free liberty in his person and property.

Whether a man be great or small, he is equally dear to me. I wish, sir, for a regular government, in order to secure and protect those honest citizens who have been distinguished—I mean the industrious farmer and planter. I wish them to be protected in the enjoyment of their honestly and industriously acquired property. I wish commerce to be fully protected and encouraged, that the people may have an opportunity of disposing of their

SOURCE: Edmund Pendleton in Jonathan Elliot, Comp., *The Debates in the Several State Conventions on the Adoption of the Federal Constitution as Recommended by the General Convention at Philadelphia*, 2nd ed., pp. 295–296 (Philadelphia: Lippincott, 1896).

crops at market, and of procuring such supplies as they may be in want of. I presume that there can be no political happiness, unless industry be cherished and protected, and property secured. Suppose a poor man becomes rich by honest labor, and increases the public stock of wealth: shall his reward be the loss of that liberty he set out with? Will you take away every stimulus to industry, by declaring that he shall not retain the fruits of it? The idea of the poor becoming rich by assiduity is not mere fancy. I am old enough, and have had sufficient experience, to know the effects of it. I have often known persons, commencing in life without any other stock but industry and economy, by the mere efforts of these, rise to opulence and wealth. This could not have been the case without a government to protect their industry. In my mind the true principle of republicanism, and the greatest security of liberty, is regular government. Perhaps I may not be a republican, but this is my idea. In reviewing the history of the world, shall we find an instance where any society retained its liberty without government? As I before hinted, the smallest society in extent, to the greatest empire, can only be preserved by a regular government, to suppress that faction and turbulence so natural to many of our species. What do men do with those passions when they come into society? Do they leave them? No; they bring them with them. These passions, which they thus bring into society, will produce disturbances, which, without any check, will overturn it.

16 FROM   *James Madison*
The Federalist Papers, No. 39

If we resort for a criterion to the different principles on which different forms of government are established, we may define a republic to be, or at least may bestow that name on, a govern-

SOURCE: James Madison in *The Federalist Papers*, No. 39, pp. 242–250 (New York: Random House, Inc., Modern Library Edition, 1941).

ment which derives all its powers directly or indirectly from the great body of the people, and is administered by persons holding their offices during pleasure, for a limited period, or during good behavior. It is *essential* to such a government that it be derived from the great body of the society, not from an inconsiderable proportion, or a favored class of it; otherwise a handful of tyrannical nobles, exercising their oppressions by a delegation of their powers, might aspire to the rank of republicans, and claim for their government the honorable title of republic. It is *sufficient* for such a government that the persons administering it be appointed, either directly or indirectly, by the people; and that they hold their appointments by either of the tenures just specified; otherwise every government in the United States, as well as every other popular government that has been or can be well organized or well executed, would be degraded from the republican character. According to the constitution of every State in the Union, some or other of the officers of government are appointed indirectly only by the people. According to most of them, the chief magistrate himself is so appointed. And according to one, this mode of appointment is extended to one of the coördinate branches of the legislature. According to all the constitutions, also, the tenure of the highest offices is extended to a definite period; and in many instances, both within the legislative and executive departments, to a period of years. According to the provisions of most of the constitutions, again, as well as according to the most respectable and received opinions on the subject, the members of the judiciary department are to retain their offices by the firm tenure of good behavior.

On comparing the Constitution planned by the convention with the standard here fixed, we perceive at once that it is, in the most rigid sense, conformable to it. The House of Representatives, like that of one branch at least of all the State legislatures, is elected immediately by the great body of the people. The Senate, like the present Congress, and the Senate of Maryland, derives its appointment indirectly from the people. The President is indirectly derived from the choice of the people, according to the example in most of the States. Even the judges with all other officers of the Union, will, as in the several States, be the choice, though a remote choice, of the people themselves. The duration of the appointments is equally conformable to the republican standard, and to the model of State constitutions. The House of Representatives is periodically elective, as in all the States; and for the period of two years, as in the State of South Carolina. The Senate is elective, for the period of six years; which is but one year more than the period of the Senate of Maryland, and but two more than that of the Senates of New York and Virginia. The President is to continue in office for the period of four years; as in New York and Delaware the chief magistrate is elected for three years, and in South Carolina for two years In the other States the election is annual. In several of the States, however, no consitutional provision is made for the impeachment of the chief magistrate. And in Delaware and Virginia he is not impeachable till out of office. The President of the United States is impeachable at any time during his continuance in office. The tenure by which the judges are to hold their places, is, as it unquestionably ought to be, that of good behavior. The tenure of the ministerial offices generally, will be a subject of legal regulation, conformably to the reason of the case and the example of the State constitutions.

Could any further proof be required of the republican complexion of this system, the most decisive one might be found in its absolute prohibition of titles of nobility, both under the federal and the State governments; and in its express guaranty of the republican form to each of the latter. . . .

17 FROM   *James Madison*
The Federalist Papers, No. 10

Among the numerous advantages promised by a well-constructed Union, none deserves to be more accurately developed than its tendency to break and control the violence of faction.

SOURCE: James Madison in *The Federalist Papers*, No. 10, pp. 53–58 (New York: Random House, Inc., Modern Library Edition, 1941).

The friend of popular governments never finds himself so much alarmed for their character and fate, as when he contemplates their propensity to this dangerous vice. He will not fail, therefore, to set a due value on any plan which, without violating the principles to which he is attached, provides a proper cure for it. The instability, injustice, and confusion introduced into the public councils, have, in truth, been the mortal diseases under which popular governments have everywhere perished; as they continue to be the favorite and fruitful topics from which the adversaries to liberty derive their most specious declamations. The valuable improvements made by the American constitutions on the popular models, both ancient and modern, cannot certainly be too much admired; but it would be an unwarrantable partiality, to contend that they have as effectually obviated the danger on this side, as was wished and expected. Complaints are everywhere heard from our most considerate and virtuous citizens, equally the friends of public and private faith, and of public and personal liberty, that our governments are too unstable, that the public good is disregarded in the conflicts of rival parties, and that measures are too often decided, not according to the rules of justice and the rights of the minor party, but by the superior force of an interested and overbearing majority. However anxiously we may wish that these complaints had no foundation, the evidence of known facts will not permit us to deny that they are in some degree true. It will be found, indeed, on a candid review of our situation, that some of the distresses under which we labor have been erroneously charged on the operation of our governments; but it will be found, at the same time, that other causes will not alone account for many of our heaviest misfortunes; and, particularly, for that prevailing and increasing distrust of public engagements, and alarm for private rights, which are echoed from one end of the continent to the other. These must be chiefly, if not wholly, effects of the unsteadiness and injustice with which a factious spirit has tainted our public administrations.

By a faction, I understand a number of citizens, whether amounting to a majority or minority of the whole, who are united and actuated by some common impulse of passion, or of interest, adverse to the rights of other citizens, or to the permanent and aggregate interests of the community.

There are two methods of curing the mischiefs of faction: the one, by removing its causes; the other, by controlling its effects.

There are again two methods of removing the causes of faction: the one, by destroying the liberty which is essential to its existence; the other, by giving to every citizen the same opinions, the same passions, and the same interests.

It could never be more truly said than of the first remedy, that it was worse than the disease. Liberty is to faction what air is to fire, an aliment without which it instantly expires. But it could not be less folly to abolish liberty, which is essential to political life, because it nourishes faction, than it would be to wish the annihilation of air, which is essential to animal life, because it imparts to fire its destructive agency.

The second expedient is as impracticable as the first would be unwise. As long as the reason of man continues fallible, and he is at liberty to exercise it, different opinions will be formed. As long as the connection subsists between his reason and his self-love, his opinions and his passions will have a reciprocal influence on each other; and the former will be the objects to which the latter will attach themselves. The diversity in the faculties of men, from which the rights of property originate, is not less an insuperable obstacle to a uniformity of interests. The protection of these faculties is the first object of government. From the protection of different and unequal faculties of acquiring property, the possession of different degrees and kinds of property immediately results; and from the influence of these on the sentiments and views of the respective proprietors, ensues a division of the society into different interests and parties.

The latent causes of faction are thus sown in the nature of man; and we see them everywhere brought into different degrees of activity, according to the different circumstances of civil society. A zeal for different opinions concerning religion, concerning government, and many other points, as well of speculation as of practice; an attachment to different leaders ambitiously contending for pre-eminence and power; or to persons of other descriptions whose fortunes have been interesting to the human passions, have, in turn, divided mankind into parties, inflamed them with mutual animosity, and rendered them much more disposed to vex and oppress each other than to co-operate for their common good. So strong is this propensity of mankind to fall into mutual animosities, that where no substantial occasion presents itself, the most frivolous and fanciful distinctions have been sufficient to kindle their unfriendly passions and excite their most violent conflicts. But the most common and durable source of factions has been the various and unequal distribution of property. Those who hold and those who are without property have ever formed distinct interests in society. Those who are creditors, and those who are debtors, fall under a like discrimination. A landed interest, a manufacturing interest, a mercantile interest, a moneyed interest, with many lesser interests, grow up of necessity in civilized nations, and divide them into different classes, actuated by different sentiments and views. The regulation of these various and interfering interests forms the principal task of modern legislation, and involves the spirit of party and faction in the necessary and ordinary operations of the government.

No man is allowed to be a judge in his own cause, because his interest would certainly bias his judgment, and, not improbably, corrupt his integrity. With equal, nay with greater reason, a body of men are unfit to be both judges and parties at the same time; yet what are many of the most important acts of legislation, but so many judicial determinations, not indeed concerning the rights of single persons, but concerning the rights of large bodies of citizens? And what are the different classes of legislators but advocates and parties to the causes which they determine? Is a law proposed concerning private debts? It is a question to which the creditors are parties on one side and the debtors on the other. Justice ought to hold the balance between them. Yet the parties are, and must be, themselves the judges; and the most numerous party, or, in other words, the most powerful faction must be expected to prevail. Shall domestic manufactures be encouraged, and in what degree, by restrictions on foreign manufactures? are questions which would be differently decided by the landed and the manufacturing classes, and probably by neither with a sole regard to justice and the public good. The apportionment of taxes on the various descriptions of property is an act which seems to require the most exact impartiality; yet there is, perhaps, no legislative act in which greater opportunity and temptation are given to a predominant party to trample on the rules of justice. Every shilling with which they overburden the inferior number, is a shilling saved to their own pockets.

It is in vain to say that enlightened statesmen will be able to adjust these clashing interests, and render them all subservient to the public good. Enlightened statesmen will not always be at the helm. Nor, in many cases, can such an adjustment be made at all without taking into view indirect and remote considerations, which will rarely prevail over the immediate interest which one party may find in disregarding the rights of another or the good of the whole.

The inference to which we are brought is, that the *causes* of faction cannot be removed, and that relief is only to be sought in the means of controlling its *effects*.

If a faction consists of less than a majority, relief is supplied by the republican principle, which enables the majority to defeat its sinister views by regular vote. It may clog the administration, it may convulse the society; but it will be unable to execute and mask its violence under the forms of the Constitution. When a majority is included in a faction, the form of popular government, on the other hand, enables it to sacrifice to its ruling passion or interest both the public good and the rights of other citizens. To secure the public good and private rights against the danger of such a faction, and at the same time to preserve the spirit and the form of popular government, is then the great object to which our inquiries are directed. Let me add that it is the great desideratum by which this form of government can be rescued from the opprobrium under which it has so long labored, and be recommended to the esteem and adoption of mankind.

THE STRUCTURAL PROBLEM:
THE PROPER SIZE
FOR A REPUBLIC

At the time that Americans wrote their first constitutions, conventional political wisdom taught that republics could only work in small territorial units inhabited by citizens with similar interests and outlooks who could reach agreements peacefully and harmoniously and could keep close tabs on their rulers. The lessons of history, reinforced by fear of distant authority and the tendency for the semi-independent colonies to assume sovereign power after the Declaration of Independence resulted in a loose Confederation and weak central government that conformed to republican theory.

The defects of this arrangement, however, forced many Americans to rethink basic assumptions about the proper size for a republic. In the following selections, advocates of the Federal Constitution explain why they believe that free government in the United States, a large and diverse society, would have a fairer chance if power were shifted from the states to the nation. By enlarging the political arena to include many diverse interests in the nation, Madison argued, it might be possible to prevent factions, analyzed in the preceding selection from Federalist No. 10, from destroying liberty since each group would jealously guard its interests against others and none would be strong enough to get its way without respecting rivals. Within the states, however, Madison believed that tyrannical majorities or minorities could command sufficient strength to abuse power. This radical rejection of local control as the best safeguard of individual liberty did not convince everyone. Critics of the Constitution, as the first set of selections indicate, held fast to the traditional view expressed by a Massachusetts citizen who said: "The idea of an uncompounded republick, on an average one thousand miles in length, and eight-hundred in breadth . . . is an absurdity and contrary to the whole experience of mankind."

ANTI-CONSTITUTIONALISTS

18 FROM *Anonymous Letters of Agrippa*

. . . It is the opinion of the ablest writers on the subject, that no extensive empire can be governed upon republican principles, and that such a government will degenerate to a despotism, unless it be made up of a confederacy of small states, each having the full powers of internal regulation. This is precisely the principle which has hitherto preserved our freedom. No instance can be found of any free government of considerable extent which has been supported upon any other plan. Large and consolidated empires may indeed dazzle the eyes of a distant spectator with their splendour, but if examined more nearly are always found to be full of misery. The reason is obvious. In large states the same principles of legislation will not apply to all the parts. The inhabitants of warmer climates are more dissolute in their manners, and less industrious, than in colder countries. A degree of severity is, therefore, necessary with one which would cramp the spirit of the other. We accordingly find that the very great empires have always been despotick. They have indeed tried to remedy the inconveniences to which the people were exposed by local regulations; but these contrivances have never answered the end. The laws not being made by the people, who felt the inconveniences, did not suit their circumstances. It is under such tyranny that the Spanish provinces languish, and such would be our misfortune and degradation, if we should submit to have the concerns of the whole empire managed by one legislature.

SOURCE: "Letters of Agrippa," in Paul L. Ford, Ed., *Essays on the Constitution of the United States, 1787–1788,* pp. 64–65 (Brooklyn, N.Y.: Brooklyn Historical Printing Club, 1892).

To promote the happiness of the people it is necessary that there should be local laws; and it is necessary that those laws should be made by the representatives of those who are immediately subject to the want of them. By endeavouring to suit both extremes, both are injured.

It is impossible for one code of laws to suit Georgia and Massachusetts. They must, therefore, legislate for themselves. Yet there is, I believe, not one point of legislation that is not surrendered in the proposed plan. Questions of every kind respecting property are determinable in a continental court, and so are all kinds of criminal causes. The continental legislature has, therefore, a right to make rules in all cases by which their judicial courts shall proceed and decide causes. No rights are reserved to the citizens. The laws of Congress are in all cases to be the supreme law of the land, and paramount to the constitutions of the individual states. The Congress may institute what modes of trial they please, and no plea drawn from the constitution of any state can avail. This new system is, therefore, a consolidation of all the states into one large mass, however diverse the parts may be of which it is to be composed. The idea of an uncompounded republick, on an average one thousand miles in length, and eight hundred in breadth, and containing six millions of white inhabitants all reduced to the same standard of morals, of habits, and of laws, is in itself an absurdity, and contrary to the whole experience of mankind. The attempt made by Great Britain to introduce such a system, struck us with horrour, and when it was proposed by some theorist that we should be represented in parliament, we uniformly declared that one legislature could not represent so many different interests for the purposes of legislation and taxation. This was the leading principle of the revolution, and makes an essential article in our creed. All that part, therefore, of the new system, which relates to the internal government of the states, ought at once to be rejected.

19 FROM   *Pennsylvania Minority*
The Address and Reasons of Dissent of the Minority of
the State of Pennsylvania to Their Constituents

We dissent, first, because it is the opinion of the most celebrated writers on government, and confirmed by uniform experience, that a very extensive territory cannot be governed on the principles of freedom, otherwise than by a confederation of republics, possessing all the powers of internal government, but united in the management of their general and foreign concerns.

If any doubt could have been entertained of the truth of the foregoing principle, it has been fully removed by the concession of *Mr. Wilson,* one of the majority on this question, and who was one of the deputies in the late general convention. In justice to him, we will give his own words; they are as follows, viz.: "The extent of country for which the new constitution was required, produced another difficulty in the business of the federal convention. It is the opinion of some celebrated writers, that to a small territory, the democratical; to a middling territory (as Montesquieu had termed it), the monarchical; and to an extensive territory, the despotic form of government is best adapted. Regarding then the wide and almost unbounded jurisdiction of the United States, at first view, the hand of despotism seemed necessary to control, connect and protect it; and hence the chief embarrassment rose. For we know that although our constituents would cheerfully submit to the legislative restraints of a free government, they would spurn at every attempt to shackle them with despotic power." And again, in another part of his speech, he continues: "Is it probable that the dissolution of the State governments, and the establishment of one *consolidated empire*

SOURCE: "The Address and Reasons of Dissent of the Minority of the State of Pennsylvania to Their Constituents," in John B. McMaster and Frederick D. Stone, Eds., *Pennsylvania and the Federal Constitution,* pp. 464–465 (Philadelphia: Historical Society of Pennsylvania, 1888).

would be eligible in its nature, and satisfactory to the people in its administration? I think not, as I have given reasons to show that so extensive a territory could not be governed, connected and preserved, but by the *supremacy of despotic power.* All the exertions of the most potent emperors of Rome were not capable of keeping that empire together, which in extent was far inferior to the dominion of America."

We dissent, secondly, because the powers vested in Congress by this constitution, must necessarily annihilate and absorb the legislative, executive, and judicial powers of the several States, and produce from their ruins one consolidated government, which from the nature of things will be *an iron handed despotism,* as nothing short of the supremacy of despotic sway could connect and govern these United States under one government.

PRO-CONSTITUTIONALISTS

20 FROM   *Alexander Hamilton*
The Federalist Papers, No. 9

A firm Union will be of the utmost moment to the peace and liberty of the States, as a barrier against domestic faction and insurrection. It is impossible to read the history of the petty republics of Greece and Italy without feeling sensations of horror and disgust at the distractions with which they were continually agitated, and at the rapid succession of revolutions by which they were kept in a state of perpetual vibration between the extremes of tyranny and anarchy. If they exhibit occasional calms, these only serve as short-lived contrasts to the furious storms that are to succeed. If now and then intervals of felicity open to view, we behold them with a mixture of regret, arising from the

SOURCE: Alexander Hamilton in *The Federalist Papers,* No. 9, pp. 47–49 (New York: Random House, Inc., Modern Library Edition, 1941).

reflection that the pleasing scenes before us are soon to be over-whelmed by the tempestuous waves of sedition and party rage. If momentary rays of glory break forth from the gloom, while they dazzle us with a transient and fleeting brilliancy, they at the same time admonish us to lament that the vices of govern-ment should pervert the direction and tarnish the lustre of those bright talents and exalted endowments for which the favored soils that produced them have been so justly celebrated.

From the disorders that disfigure the annals of those republics the advocates of despotism have drawn arguments, not only against the forms of republican government, but against the very principles of civil liberty. They have decried all free government as inconsistent with the order of society, and have indulged themselves in malicious exultation over its friends and partisans. Happily for mankind, stupendous fabrics reared on the basis of liberty, which have flourished for ages, have, in a few glorious instances, refuted their gloomy sophisms. And, I trust, America will be the broad and solid foundation of other edifices, not less magnificent, which will be equally permanent monuments of their errors.

But it is not to be denied that the portraits they have sketched of republican government were too just copies of the originals from which they were taken. If it had been found impracticable to have devised models of a more perfect structure, the en-lightened friends to liberty would have been obliged to abandon the cause of that species of government as indefensible. The science of politics, however, like most other sciences, has received great improvement. The efficacy of various principles is now well understood, which were either not known at all, or imperfectly known to the ancients. The regular distribution of power into distinct departments; the introduction of legislative balances and checks; the institution of courts composed of judges holding their offices during good behavior; the representation of the people in the legislature by deputies of their own election: these are wholly new discoveries, or have made their principal progress towards perfection in modern times. They are means, and powerful means, by which the excellences of republican govern-ment may be retained and its imperfections lessened or avoided. To this catalogue of circumstances that tend to the amelioration of popular systems of civil government, I shall venture, however novel it may appear to some, to add one more, on a principle which has been made the foundation of an objection to the new Constitution; I mean the ENLARGEMENT of the ORBIT within which such systems are to resolve, either in respect to the dimensions of a single State, or to the consolidation of several smaller States into one great Confederacy. The latter is that which immediately concerns the object under consideration. It will, however, be of use to examine the principle in its application to a single State, which shall be attended to in another place.

The utility of a Confederacy, as well to suppress faction and to guard the internal tranquillity of States, as to increase their external force and security, is in reality not a new idea. It has been practised upon in different countries and ages, and has received the sanction of the most approved writers on the subjects of politics. The opponents of the plan proposed have, with great assiduity, cited and circulated the observations of Montesquieu on the necessity of a contracted territory for a republican government. But they seem not to have been apprised of the sentiments of that great man expressed in another part of his work, nor to have adverted to the consequences of the principle to which they subscribe with such ready acquiescence.

21   FROM   *James Madison*
        The Federalist Papers, No. 10

The inference to which we are brought is, that the *causes* of faction cannot be removed, and that relief is only to be sought in the means of controlling its *effects*.

If a faction consists of less than a majority, relief is supplied by the republican principle, which enables the majority to defeat its sinister views by regular vote. It may clog the adminis-

SOURCE: James Madison in *The Federalist Papers*, No. 10, pp. 57–62 (New York: Random House, Inc., Modern Library Edition, 1941).

tration, it may convulse the society; but it will be unable to execute and mask its violence under the forms of the Constitution. When a majority is included in a faction, the form of popular government, on the other hand, enables it to sacrifice to its ruling passion or interest both the public good and the rights of other citizens. To secure the public good and private rights against the danger of such a faction, and at the same time to preserve the spirit and the form of popular government, is then the great object to which our inquiries are directed. Let me add that it is the great desideratum by which this form of government can be rescued from the opprobrium under which it has so long labored, and be recommended to the esteem and adoption of mankind.

By what means is this object attainable? Evidently by one of two only. Either the existence of the same passion or interest in a majority at the same time must be prevented, or the majority, having such coexistent passion or interest, must be rendered, by their number and local situation, unable to concert and carry into effect schemes of oppression. If the impulse and the opportunity be suffered to coincide, we well know that neither moral nor religious motives can be relied on as an adequate control. They are not found to be such on the injustice and violence of individuals, and lose their efficacy in proportion to the number combined together, that is, in proportion as their efficacy becomes needful.

From this view of the subject it may be concluded that a pure democracy, by which I mean a society consisting of a small number of citizens, who assemble and administer the government in person, can admit of no cure for the mischiefs of faction. A common passion or interest will, in almost every case, be felt by a majority of the whole; a communication and concert result from the form of government itself; and there is nothing to check the inducements to sacrifice the weaker party or an obnoxious individual. Hence it is that such democracies have ever been spectacles of turbulence and contention; have ever been found incompatible with personal security or the rights of property; and have in general been as short in their lives as they have been violent in their deaths. Theoretic politicians, who have patronized this species of government, have erroneously supposed that by reducing mankind to a perfect equality in their political rights, they would, at the same time, be perfectly equalized and assimilated in their possessions, their opinions, and their passions.

A republic, by which I mean a government in which the scheme of representation takes place, opens a different prospect, and promises the cure for which we are seeking. Let us examine the points in which it varies from pure democracy, and we shall comprehend both the nature of the cure and the efficacy which it must derive from the Union.

The two great points of difference between a democracy and a republic are: first, the delegation of the government, in the latter, to a small number of citizens elected by the rest; secondly, the greater number of citizens, and greater sphere of country, over which the latter may be extended.

The effect of the first difference is, on the one hand, to refine and enlarge the public views, by passing them through the medium of a chosen body of citizens, whose wisdom may best discern the true interest of their country, and whose patriotism and love of justice will be least likely to sacrifice it to temporary or partial considerations. Under such a regulation, it may well happen that the public voice, pronounced by the representatives of the people, will be more consonant to the public good than if pronounced by the people themselves, convened for the purpose. On the other hand, the effect may be inverted. Men of factious tempers, of local prejudices, or of sinister designs, may, by intrigue, by corruption, or by other means, first obtain the suffrages, and then betray the interests, of the people. The question resulting is, whether small or extensive republics are more favorable to the election of proper guardians of the public weal; and it is clearly decided in favor of the latter by two obvious considerations:

In the first place, it is to be remarked that, however small the republic may be, the representatives must be raised to a certain number, in order to guard against the cabals of a few; and that, however large it may be, they must be limited to a certain number, in order to guard against the confusion of a multitude. Hence, the number of representatives in the two cases not being in proportion to that of the two constituents, and being proportionally greater in the small republic, it follows that, if the proportion of fit characters be not less in the large than in the small republic, the former will present a greater option, and consequently a greater probability of a fit choice.

In the next place, as each representative will be chosen by a greater number of citizens in the large than in the small republic, it will be more difficult for unworthy candidates to practise with success the vicious arts by which elections are too often carried; and the suffrages of the people being more free, will be more likely to centre in men who possess the most attractive merit and the most diffusive and established characters.

It must be confessed that in this, as in most other cases, there is a mean, on both sides of which inconveniences will be found to lie. By enlarging too much the number of electors, you render the representative too little acquainted with all their local circumstances and lesser interests; as by reducing it too much, you render him unduly attached to these, and too little fit to comprehend and pursue great and national objects. The federal Constitution forms a happy combination in this respect; the great and aggregate interests being referred to the national, the local and particular to the State legislatures.

The other point of difference is, the greater number of citizens and extent of territory which may be brought within the compass of republican than of democratic government; and it is this circumstance principally which renders factious combinations less to be dreaded in the former than in the latter. The smaller the society, the fewer probably will be the distinct parties and interests composing it; the fewer the distinct parties and interests, the more frequently will a majority be found of the same party; and the smaller the number of individuals composing a majority, and the smaller the compass within which they are placed, the more easily will they concert and execute their plans of oppression. Extend the sphere and you take in a greater variety of parties and interests; you make it less probable that a majority of the whole will have a common motive to invade the rights of other citizens; or if such a common motive exists, it will be more difficult for all who feel it to discover their own strength, and to act in unison with each other. Besides other impediments, it may be remarked that, where there is a consciousness of unjust or dishonorable purposes, communication is always checked by distrust in proportion to the number whose concurrence is necessary.

Hence, it clearly appears, that the same advantage which a republic has over a democracy, in controlling the effects of faction, is enjoyed by a large over a small republic,—is enjoyed by the Union over the States composing it. Does the advantage consist in the substitution of representatives whose enlightened views and virtuous sentiments render them superior to local prejudices and to schemes of injustice? It will not be denied that the representation of the Union will be most likely to possess these requisite endowments. Does it consist in the greater security afforded by a greater variety of parties, against the event of any one party being able to outnumber and oppress the rest? In an equal degree does the increased variety of parties comprised within the Union, increase this security. Does it, in fine, consist in the greater obstacles opposed to the concert and accomplishment of the secret wishes of an unjust and interested majority? Here, again, the extent of the Union gives it the most palpable advantage.

The influence of factious leaders may kindle a flame within their particular States, but will be unable to spread a general conflagration through the other States. A religious sect may degenerate into a political faction in a part of the Confederacy; but the variety of sects dispersed over the entire face of it must secure the national councils against any danger from that source. A rage for paper money, for an abolition of debts, for an equal division of property, or for any other improper or wicked project, will be less apt to pervade the whole body of the Union than a particular member of it; in the same proportion as such a malady is more likely to taint a particular county or district, than an entire State.

In the extent and proper structure of the Union, therefore, we behold a republican remedy for the diseases most incident to republican government. And according to the degree of pleasure and pride we feel in being republicans, ought to be our zeal in cherishing the spirit and supporting the character of Federalists.

22 FROM   *James Madison*
          The Federalist Papers, No. 14

. . . Hearken not to the voice which petulantly tells you that the form of government recommended for your adoption is a novelty in the political world; that it has never yet had a place in the theories of the wildest projectors; that it rashly attempts what it is impossible to accomplish. No, my countrymen, shut your ears against this unhallowed language. Shut your hearts against the poison which it conveys; the kindred blood which flows in the veins of American citizens, the mingled blood which they have shed in defence of their sacred rights, consecrate their Union, and excite horror at the idea of their becoming aliens, rivals, enemies. And if novelties are to be shunned, believe me, the most alarming of all novelties, the most wild of all projects, the most rash of all attempts, is that of rending us in pieces, in order to preserve our liberties and promote our happiness. But why is the experiment of an extended republic to be rejected, merely because it may comprise what is new? Is it not the glory of the people of America, that, whilst they have paid a decent regard to the opinions of former times and other nations, they have not suffered a blind veneration for antiquity, for custom, or for names, to overrule the suggestions of their own good sense, the knowledge of their own situation, and the lessons of their own experience? To this manly spirit, posterity will be indebted for the possession, and the world for the example, of the numerous innovations displayed on the American theatre, in favor of private rights and public happiness. Had no important step been taken by the leaders of the Revolution for which a precedent could not be discovered, no government established of which an exact model did not present itself, the people of the United States might, at this moment, have been numbered

SOURCE: James Madison in *The Federalist Papers,* No. 14, pp. 84–85 (New York: Random House, Inc., Modern Library Edition, 1941).

among the melancholy victims of misguided councils, must at best have been laboring under the weight of some of those forms which have crushed the liberties of the rest of mankind. Happily for America, happily, we trust, for the whole human race, they pursued a new and more noble course. They accomplished a revolution which has no parallel in the annals of human society. They reared the fabrics of governments which have no model on the face of the globe. They formed the design of a great Confederacy, which it is incumbent on their successors to improve and perpetuate. If their works betray imperfections, we wonder at the fewness of them. If they erred most in the structure of the Union, this was the work most difficult to be executed; this is the work which has been new modelled by the act of your convention, and it is that act on which you are now to deliberate and to decide.

CONSOLIDATION OR FEDERALISM?

Since it was an axiom of contemporary political thought that sovereignty or ultimate power was by definition indivisible, the Federal system designed by the founding fathers to divide power between the states and the nation appeared impractical to some and incomprehensible to others. Anti-Constitutionalists, holding to a traditional view, warned that a shift in power from the states to the nation would consolidate power at the center and undermine local government. The power to tax, they argued, involved the power to destroy; by giving the nation that authority, the states would lose an indispensable basis of their sovereignty. Because federalism was a new idea and clashed with accepted notions about sovereignty and with existing constitutional arrangements, the founding fathers encountered great difficulty convincing citizens of the wisdom of a scheme that later proved to be one of their most successful inventions. They reasoned that sovereignty resided not in governments but in the people who were the source of all power, whether exercised by the states or the nation. The people, therefore, could delegate some powers to the states, others to the nation, and reserve still others to themselves. Thus under the Federal Constitution both the states and the nation had the power to tax but that authority could only be exercised by the representatives of the people in the state legislatures and Congress. For these reasons, pro-Constitutionalists thought federalism practical. They also believed that it offered the best hope of preserving regional diversity while achieving national strength and unity.

ANTI-CONSTITUTIONALISTS

23 FROM *Patrick Henry*
The Virginia Convention

It will be necessary for this Convention to have a faithful historical detail of the facts that preceded the session of the Federal Convention, and the reasons that actuated its members in proposing an entire alteration of government, and to demonstrate the dangers that awaited us. If they were of such awful magnitude as to warrant a proposal so extremely perilous as this, I must assert that this Convention has an absolute right to a thorough discovery of every circumstance relative to this great event. And here I would make this inquiry of those worthy characters who composed a part of the late Federal Convention. I am sure they were fully impressed with the necessity of forming a great consolidated government, instead of a confederation. That this is a consolidated government is demonstrably clear; and the danger of such a government is, to my mind, very striking. I have the highest veneration for those gentlemen; but, sir, give me leave to demand, What right had they to say, *We, the People?* My political curiosity, exclusive of my anxious solicitude for the public welfare, leads me to ask, Who authorized them to speak the language of, *We, the People,* instead of, *We, the States?* States are the characteristics and the soul of a confederation. If the States be not the agents of this compact, it must be one great consolidated National Government, of the people of all the States. . . .

SOURCE: Patrick Henry in Jonathan Elliot, Comp., *The Debates in the Several State Conventions on the Adoption of the Federal Constitution as Recommended by the General Convention at Philadelphia,* 2nd ed., III, p. 22 (Philadelphia: Lippincott, 1896).

24 FROM *Richard H. Lee*
Letters from the Federal Farmer to the Republican

. . . It is necessary, therefore, to examine the extent, and the probable operations of some of those extensive powers proposed to be vested in this government. These powers, legislative, executive, and judicial, respect internal as well as external objects. Those respecting external objects, as all foreign concerns, commerce, imposts, all causes arising on the seas, peace and war, and Indian affairs, can be lodged no where else, with any propriety, but in this government. Many powers that respect internal objects ought clearly to be lodged in it; as those to regulate trade between the states, weights and measures, the coin or current monies, post-offices, naturalization, &c. These powers may be exercised without essentially effecting the internal police of the respective states: But powers to lay and collect internal taxes, to form the militia, to make bankrupt laws, and to decide on appeals, questions arising on the internal laws of the respective states, are of a very serious nature, and carry with them almost all other powers. These taken in connection with the others, and powers to raise armies and build navies, proposed to be lodged in this government, appear to me to comprehend all the essential powers in this community, and those which will be left to the states will be of no great importance.

A power to lay and collect taxes at discretion, is, in itself, of very great importance. By means of taxes, the government may command the whole or any part of the subject's property. Taxes may be of various kinds; but there is a strong distinction between external and internal taxes. External taxes are import duties, which are laid on imported goods; they may usually be collected in a few seaport towns, and of a few individuals, though ulti-

SOURCE: Richard H. Lee, "Letters from the Federal Farmer to the Republican," in Paul L. Ford, Ed., *Pamphlets on the Constitution of the United States,* pp. 300–302 (New York: Brooklyn Historical Printing Club, 1888).

mately paid by the consumer; a few officers can collect them, and they can be carried no higher than trade will bear, or smuggling permit—that in the very nature of commerce, bounds are set to them. But internal taxes, as poll and land taxes, excises, duties on all written instruments, &c. may fix themselves on every person and species of property in the community; they may be carried to any lengths, and in proportion as they are extended, numerous officers must be employed to assess them, and to enforce the collection of them. In the United Netherlands the general government has compleat powers, as to external taxation; but as to internal taxes, it makes requisitions on the provinces. Internal taxation in this country is more important, as the country is so very extensive. As many assessors and collectors of federal taxes will be above three hundred miles from the seat of the federal government as will be less. Besides, to lay and collect taxes, in this extensive country, must require a great number of congressional ordinances, immediately operating upon the body of the people; these must continually interfere with the state laws, and thereby produce disorder and general dissatis-faction, till the one system of laws or the other, operating on the same subjects, shall be abolished. These ordinances alone, to say nothing of those respecting the militia, coin, commerce, federal judiciary, &c., &c. will probably soon defeat the operations of the state laws and governments.

25 FROM *Robert Yates*
The New York Journal and Weekly Register

How far the power to lay and collect duties and excises, may operate to dissolve the state governments, and oppress the people, it is impossible to say. It would assist us much in forming a just opinion on this head, to consider the various objects to which

SOURCE: Robert Yates in *The New York Journal and Weekly Register* (December 27, 1787).

this kind of taxes extend, in European nations, and the infinity of laws they have passed respecting them. Perhaps, if leisure will permit, this may be essayed in some future paper. . . .

This power, exercised without limitation, will introduce itself into every corner of the city, and country—It will wait upon the ladies at their toilett, and will not leave them in any of their domestic concerns; it will accompany them to the ball, the play, and the assembly; it will go with them when they visit, and will, on all occasions, sit beside them in their carriages, nor will it desert them even at church; it will enter the house of every gentleman, watch over his cellar, wait upon his cook in the kitchen, follow the servants into the parlour, preside over the table, and note down all he eats or drinks; it will attend him to his bedchamber, and watch him while he sleeps; it will take cognizance of the professional man in his office, or his study; it will watch the merchant in the counting-house, or in his store; it will follow the mechanic to his shop, and in his work, and will haunt him in his family, and in his bed; it will be a constant companion of the industrious farmer in all his labour, it will be with him in the house, and in the field, observe the toil of his hands, and the sweat of his brow; it will penetrate into the most obscure cottage; and finally, it will light upon the head of every person in the United States. To all these different classes of people, and in all these circumstances, in which it will attend them, the language in which it will address them will be GIVE! GIVE!

A power that has such latitude, which reaches every person in the community in every conceivable circumstance, and lays hold of every species of property they possess, and which has no bounds set to it, but the discretion of those who exercise it. I say, such a power must necessarily, from its very nature, swallow up all the power of the state governments.

I shall add but one other observation on this head, which is this—It appears to me a solecism, for two men, or bodies of men, to have unlimited power respecting the same object. It contradicts the scripture maxim which saith, "no man can serve two masters," the one power or the other must prevail, or else they will destroy each other, and neither of them effect their purpose. It may be compared to two mechanic powers, acting upon the same body in opposite directions, the consequence would be, if the powers

were equal, the body would remain in a state of rest, or if the
force of the one was superior to that of the other, the stronger
would prevail, and overcome the resistance of the weaker.

PRO-CONSTITUTIONALISTS

26 FROM   *Edmund Pendleton*
            The Virginia Convention

But we are told that there will be a war between the two bodies
equally our representatives, and that the state government will be
destroyed, and consolidated into the general government. I
stated before, that this could not be so. The two governments act
in different manners, and for different purposes—the general government in great national concerns, in which we are interested in
common with other members of the Union; the state legislature
in our mere local concerns. Is it true, or merely imaginary, that
the state legislatures will be confined to the care of bridges and
roads? I think that they are still possessed of the highest powers.
Our dearest rights,—life, liberty, and property,—as Virginians, are
still in the hands of our state legislature. If they prove too feeble
to protect us, we resort to the aid of the general government for
security. The true distinction is, that the two governments are
established for different purposes, and act on different objects;
so that, notwithstanding what the worthy gentleman said, I believe
I am still correct, and insist that, if each power is confined within
its proper bounds, and to its proper objects, an interference can
never happen. Being for two different purposes, as long as they
are limited to the different objects, they can no more clash than
two parallel lines can meet. Both lay taxes, but for different pur-

SOURCE: Edmund Pendleton in Jonathan Elliot, Comp., *The Debates in
the Several State Conventions on the Adoption of the Federal Constitution
as Recommended by the General Convention at Philadelphia*, 2nd ed., III, p.
301 (Philadelphia: Lippincott, 1896).

poses. The same officers may be used by both governments, which will prevent a number of inconveniences. If an invasion, or insurrection, or other misfortune, should make it necessary for the general government to interpose, this will be for the general purposes of the Union, and for the manifest interest of the states.

I mentioned formerly that it would never be the interest of the general government to destroy the state governments. From these it will derive great strength: for if *they* be possessed of power, they will assist *it;* if *they* become feeble, or decay, the general government must likewise become weak, or moulder away.

27 FROM   *James Madison*
The Federalist Papers, No. 39

First.—In order to ascertain the real character of the government, it may be considered in relation to the foundation on which it is to be established; to the sources from which its ordinary powers are to be drawn; to the operation of those powers; to the extent of them; and to the authority by which future changes in the government are to be introduced.

On examining the first relation, it appears, on one hand, that the Constitution is to be founded on the assent and ratification of the people of America, given by deputies elected for the special purpose; but, on the other, that this assent and ratification is to be given by the people, not as individuals composing one entire nation, but as composing the distinct and independent States to which they respectively belong. It is to be the assent and ratification of the several States, derived from the supreme authority in each State,—the authority of the people themselves. The act, therefore, establishing the Constitution, will not be a *national,* but a *federal* act.

SOURCE: James Madison in *The Federalist Papers,* No. 39, pp. 246–250 (New York: Random House, Inc., Modern Library Edition, 1941).

That it will be a federal and not a national act, as these terms are understood by the objectors; the act of the people, as forming so many independent States, not as forming one aggregate nation, is obvious from this single consideration, that it is to result neither from the decision of a *majority* of the people of the Union, nor from that of a *majority* of the States. It must result from the *unanimous* assent of the several States that are parties to it, differing no otherwise from their ordinary assent than in its being expressed, not by the legislative authority, but by that of the people themselves. Were the people regarded in this transaction as forming one nation, the will of the majority of the whole people of the United States would bind the minority, in the same manner as the majority in each State must bind the minority; and the will of the majority must be determined either by a comparison of the individual votes, or by considering the will of the majority of the States as evidence of the will of a majority of the people of the United States. Neither of these rules has been adopted. Each State, in ratifying the Constitution, is considered as a sovereign body, independent of all others, and only to be bound by its own voluntary act. In this relation, then, the new Constitution will, if established, be a *federal,* and not a *national* constitution.

The next relation is, to the sources from which the ordinary powers of government are to be derived. The House of Representatives will derive its powers from the people of America; and the people will be represented in the same proportion, and on the same principle, as they are in the legislature of a particular State. So far the government is *national,* not *federal.* The Senate, on the other hand, will derive its powers from the States, as political and coequal societies; and these will be represented on the principle of equality in the Senate, as they now are in the existing Congress. So far the government is *federal,* not *national.* The executive power will be derived from a very compound source. The immediate election of the President is to be made by the States in their political characters. The votes allotted to them are in a compound ratio, which considers them partly as distinct and coequal societies, partly as unequal members of the same society. The eventual election, again, is to be made by that branch of the legislature which consists of the national representatives; but in this particular act they are to be thrown into the form of individual delegations, from so many distinct and coequal bodies politic. From this aspect of the government, it appears to be of a mixed character, presenting at least as many *federal* as *national* features.

The difference between a federal and national government, as it relates to the *operation of the government,* is supposed to consist in this, that in the former the powers operate on the political bodies composing the Confederacy, in their political capacities; in the latter, on the individual citizens composing the nation, in their individual capacities. On trying the Constitution by this criterion, it falls under the *national,* not the *federal.*character; though perhaps not so completely as has been understood. In several cases, and particularly in the trial of controversies to which States may be parties, they must be viewed and proceeded against in their collective and political capacities only. So far the national countenance of the government on this side seems to be disfigured by a few federal features. But this blemish is perhaps unavoidable in any plan; and the operation of the government on the people, in their individual capacities, in its ordinary and most essential proceedings, may, on the whole, designate it, in this relation, a *national* government.

But if the government be national with regard to the *operation* of its powers, it changes its aspect again when we contemplate it in relation to the extent of its powers. The idea of a national government involves in it, not only an authority over the individual citizens, but an indefinite supremacy over all persons and things, so far as they are objects of lawful government. Among a people consolidated into one nation, this supremacy is completely vested in the national legislature. Among communities united for particular purposes, it is vested partly in the general and partly in the municipal legislatures. In the former case, all local authorities are subordinate to the supreme; and may be controlled, directed, or abolished by it at pleasure. In the latter, the local or municipal authorities form distinct and independent portions of the supremacy, no more subject, within their respective spheres, to the general authority, than the general authority is subject to them, within its own sphere. In this relation, then, the proposed government cannot be deemed a *national* one; since its jurisdiction extends to certain enumerated objects only, and leaves to the several States a residuary and inviolable sovereignty over all other objects. It is true that in controversies relating to the boundary between the two jurisdictions, the tribunal which is ultimately to decide, is to be established under the general government. But this does not change the principle of the case. The decision is to be impartially made, according to the rules of the Constitution; and all the usual and most effectual precautions are taken to secure this impartiality. Some such tribunal is clearly essential to prevent an appeal to the sword and a dissolution of the compact; and that it ought to be established under the general rather than under the local governments, or, to speak more properly, that it could be safely established under the first alone, is a position not likely to be combated.

If we try the Constitution by its last relation to the authority by which amendments are to be made, we find it neither wholly *national* nor wholly *federal*. Were it wholly national, the supreme and ultimate authority would reside in the *majority* of the people of the Union; and this authority would be competent at all times, like that of a majority of every national society, to alter or abolish its established government. Were it wholly federal, on the other hand, the concurrence of each State in the Union would be essential to every alteration that would be binding on all. The mode provided by the plan of the convention is not founded on either of these principles. In requiring more than a majority, and particularly in computing the proportion by *States,* not by *citizens,* it departs from the *national* and advances towards the *federal* character; in rendering the concurrence of less than the whole number of States sufficient, it loses again the *federal* and partakes of the *national* character.

The proposed Constitution, therefore, is in strictness, neither a national nor a federal Constitution, but a composition of both. In its foundation it is federal, not national; in the sources from which the ordinary powers of the government are drawn, it is partly federal and partly national; in the operation of these powers, it is national, not federal; in the extent of them, again, it is federal, not national; and, finally, in the authoritative mode of introducing amendments, it is neither wholly federal nor wholly national.

28 FROM *Alexander Hamilton*
The Federalist Papers, No. 32

Although I am of opinion that there would be no real danger
of the consequences which seem to be apprehended to the State
governments from a power in the Union to control them in the
levies of money, because I am persuaded that the sense of the
people, the extreme hazard of provoking the resentments of the
State governments, and a conviction of the utility and necessity of
local administrations for local purposes, would be a complete
barrier against the oppressive use of such a power; yet I am willing here to allow, in its full extent, the justness of the reasoning
which requires that the individual States should possess an independent and uncontrollable authority to raise their own revenues
for the supply of their own wants. And making this concession,
I affirm that (with the sole exception of duties on imports and
exports) they would, under the plan of the convention, retain that
authority in the most absolute and unqualified sense; and that an
attempt on the part of the national government to abridge them
in the exercise of it, would be a violent assumption of power,
unwarranted by any article or clause of its Constitution.

An entire consolidation of the States into one complete national
sovereignty would imply an entire subordination of the parts; and
whatever powers might remain in them, would be altogether dependent on the general will. But as the plan of the convention
aims only at a partial union or consolidation, the State governments would clearly retain all the rights of sovereignty which they
before had, and which were not, by that act, *exclusively* delegated
to the United States. This exclusive delegation, or rather this
alienation, of State sovereignty, would only exist in three cases:
where the Constitution in express terms granted an exclusive
authority to the Union; where it granted in one instance an au-

SOURCE: Alexander Hamilton in *The Federalist Papers*, No. 32, pp. 193–
197 (New York: Random House, Inc., Modern Library Edition, 1941).

thority to the Union, and in another prohibited the States from exercising the like authority; and where it granted an authority to the Union, to which a similar authority in the States would be absolutely and totally *contradictory* and *repugnant*. I use these terms to distinguish this last case from another which might appear to resemble it, but which would, in fact, be essentially different; I mean where the exercise of a concurrent jurisdiction might be productive of occasional interferences in the *policy* of any branch of administration, but would not imply any direct contradiction or repugnancy in point of constitutional authority. These three cases of exclusive jurisdiction in the federal government may be exemplified by the following instances: The last clause but one in the eighth section of the first article provides expressly that Congress shall exercise *"exclusive legislation"* over the district to be appropriated as the seat of government. This answers to the first case. The first clause of the same section empowers Congress *"to lay and collect taxes, duties, imposts, and excises";* and the second clause of the tenth section of the same article declares that, *"no State shall,* without the consent of Congress, *lay any imposts or duties on imports or exports,* except for the purpose of executing its inspection laws."* Hence would result an exclusive power in the Union to lay duties on imports and exports, with the particular exception mentioned; but this power is abridged by another clause, which declares that no tax or duty shall be laid on articles exported from any State; in consequence of which qualification, it now only extends to the *duties on imports.* This answers to the second case. The third will be found in that clause which declares that Congress shall have power "to establish an UNIFORM RULE of naturalization throughout the United States." This must necessarily be exclusive; because if each State had power to prescribe a DISTINCT RULE, there could not be a UNIFORM RULE.

A case which may perhaps be thought to resemble the latter, but which is in fact widely different, affects the question immediately under consideration. I mean the power of imposing taxes on all articles other than exports and imports. This, I contend, is manifestly a concurrent and coequal authority in the United States and in the individual States. There is plainly no expression in the granting clause which makes that power *exclusive* in the Union. There is no independent clause or sentence which prohibits the States from exercising it. . . .

As to a supposition of repugnancy between the power of taxation in the States and in the Union, it cannot be supported in that sense which would be requisite to work an exclusion of the States. It is, indeed, possible that a tax might be laid on a particular article by a State which might render it *inexpedient* that thus a further tax should be laid on the same article by the Union; but it would not imply a constitutional inability to impose a further tax. The quantity of the imposition, the expediency or inexpediency of an increase on either side, would be mutually questions of prudence; but there would be involved no direct contradiction of power. The particular policy of the national and of the State systems of finance might now and then not exactly coincide, and might require reciprocal forbearances. It is not, however, a mere possibility of inconvenience in the exercise of powers, but an immediate constitutional repugnancy that can by implication alienate and extinguish a preëxisting right of sovereignty.

The necessity of a concurrent jurisdiction in certain cases results from the division of the sovereign power; and the rule that all authorities, of which the States are not explicitly divested in favor of the Union, remain with them in full vigor, is not a theoretical consequence of that division, but is clearly admitted by the whole tenor of the instrument which contains the articles of the proposed Constitution. We there find that, notwithstanding the affirmative grants of general authorities, there has been the most pointed care in those cases where it was deemed improper that the like authorities should reside in the States, to insert negative clauses prohibiting the exercise of them by the States. The tenth section of the first article consists altogether of such provisions. This circumstance is a clear indication of the sense of the convention, and furnishes a rule of interpretation out of the body of the act, which justifies the position I have advanced and refutes every hypothesis to the contrary.

REPRESENTATION

The Federal system was one principal innovation of the Federal Constitution; the system of representation was another. Popularly elected legislative bodies that accurately mirrored the interests of citizens were regarded as the cornerstone of republican government. The state constitutions framed during the Revolution attempted to achieve this by keeping constituencies relatively small and socially uniform so that all the particular interests in the state had a voice in the assembly. Annual elections further made sure that legislators faithfully represented those who elected them or faced prompt removal. The Federal Constitution significantly departed from these practices. Members of the House of Representatives, the popularly elected branch of the Federal legislature, had two-year terms and their constituencies were relatively large and socially diverse. This meant that particular interests back home might not be able to control a Congressman's vote. The framers expected Congressmen to be sensitive to local views, but they also wanted to give them some independence from local pressures so they could make laws that promoted the common good. By designing Congressional districts that were extensive, comprising diverse elements no one of which could control elections, they expected that representatives would be freer to adopt national perspectives rather than serve simply as attornies for parochial interests. The following selections reveal the fundamental differences between opponents and supporters of the Constitution over the plan of representation.

ANTI-CONSTITUTIONALISTS

29 FROM *Melancton Smith The New York Convention*

To determine whether the number of representatives proposed by this Constitution is sufficient, it is proper to examine the quali-

SOURCE: Melancton Smith in Jonathan Elliot, Comp., *The Debates in the Several State Conventions on the Adoption of the Federal Constitution as Recommended by the General Convention at Philadelphia*, 2nd ed., II, pp. 245–249 (Philadelphia: Lippincott, 1896).

fications which this house ought to possess, in order to exercise their power discreetly for the happiness of the people. The idea that naturally suggests itself to our minds, when we speak of representatives, is, that they resemble those they represent. They should be a true picture of the people, possess a knowledge of their circumstances and their wants, sympathize in all their distresses, and be disposed to seek their true interests. The knowledge necessary for the representative of a free people not only comprehends extensive political and commercial information, such as is acquired by men of refined education, who have leisure to attain to high degrees of improvement, but it should also comprehend that kind of acquaintance with the common concerns and occupations of the people, which men of the middling class of life are, in general, more competent to than those of a superior class. To understand the true commercial interests of a country, not only requires just ideas of the general commerce of the world, but also, and principally, a knowledge of the productions of your own country, and their value, what your soil is capable of producing, the nature of your manufactures, and the capacity of the country to increase both. To exercise the power of laying taxes, duties, and excises, with discretion, requires something more than an acquaintance with the abstruse parts of the system of finance. It calls for a knowledge of the circumstances and ability of the people in general—a discernment how the burdens imposed will bear upon the different classes.

From these observations results this conclusion—that the number of representatives should be so large, as that, while it embraces the men of the first class, it should admit those of the middling class of life. I am convinced that this government is so constituted that the representatives will generally be composed of the first class in the community, which I shall distinguish by the name of the *natural aristocracy* of the country. I do not mean to give offence by using this term. I am sensible this idea is treated by many gentlemen as chimerical. I shall be asked what is meant by the *natural aristocracy,* and told that no such distinction of classes of men exists among us. It is true, it is our singular felicity that we have no legal or hereditary distinctions of this kind; but still there are real differences. Every society naturally divides itself into classes. The Author of nature has bestowed on some greater capacities than others; birth, education, talents, and wealth, create distinctions among men as visible, and of as much influence, as titles, stars, and garters. In every society, men of this class will command a superior degree of respect; and if the government is so constituted as to admit but few to exercise the powers of it, it will, according to the natural course of things, be in their hands. Men in the middling class, who are qualified as representatives, will not be so anxious to be chosen as those of the first. When the number is so small, the office will be highly elevated and distinguished; the style in which the members live will probably be high; circumstances of this kind will render the place of a representative not a desirable one to sensible, substantial men, who have been used to walk in the plain and frugal paths of life.

Besides, the influence of the great will generally enable them to succeed in elections. It will be difficult to combine a district of country containing thirty or forty thousand inhabitants,—frame your election laws as you please,—in any other character, unless it be in one of conspicuous military, popular, civil, or legal talents. The great easily form associations; the poor and middling class form them with difficulty. If the elections be by plurality,—as probably will be the case in this state,—it is about certain none but the great will be chosen, for they easily unite their interests: the common people will divide, and their divisions will be promoted by the others. There will be scarcely a chance of their uniting in any other but some great man, unless in some popular demagogue, who will probably be destitute of principle. A substantial yeoman, of sense and discernment, will hardly ever be chosen. From these remarks, it appears that the government will fall into the hands of the few and the great. This will be a government of oppression. I do not mean to declaim against the great, and charge them indiscriminately with want of principle and honesty. The same passions and prejudices govern all men. The circumstances in which men are placed in a great measure give a cast to the human character. Those in middling circumstances have less temptation; they are inclined by habit, and the company with whom they associate, to set bounds to their passions and appetites. If this is not sufficient, the want of means to gratify them will be a restraint: they are obliged to employ their time in their respective callings; hence the substantial yeomanry of the country are more temperate, of better morals, and less ambition, than the great. The latter do not feel for the poor and middling class; the reasons are obvious—they are not obliged to use the same pains and labor to procure property as the other. They feel not the inconveniences arising from the payment of small sums. The great consider themselves above the common people, entitled to more respect, do not associate with them; they fancy themselves to have a right of preëminence in every thing. In short, they possess the same feelings, and are under the influence of the same motives, as an hereditary nobility. I know the idea that such a distinction exists in this country is ridiculed by some; but I am not the less apprehensive of danger from their influence on this account. Such distinctions exist all the world over, have been taken notice of by all writers on free government, and are founded in the nature of things. It has been the principal care of free governments to guard against the encroachments of the great. Common observation and experience prove the existence of such distinctions. Will any one say that there does not exist in this country the pride of family, of wealth, of talents, and that they do not command influence and respect among the common people? Congress, in their address to the inhabitants of the province of Quebec, in 1775, state this distinction in the following forcible words, quoted from the Marquis Beccaria: "In every human society there is an essay continually tending to confer on one part the height of power and happiness, and to reduce the other to the extreme of weakness and misery. The intent of good laws is to oppose this effort, and to diffuse their influence universally and equally." We ought to guard against the government being placed in the hands of this class. They cannot have that sympathy with their constituents which is necessary to connect them closely to their interests. Being in the habit of profuse living, they will be profuse in the public expenses. They find no difficulty in paying their taxes, and therefore do not feel public burdens. Besides, if they govern, they will enjoy the emoluments of the government. The middling class, from their frugal habits, and feeling themselves the public burdens, will be careful how they increase them.

But I may be asked, Would you exclude the first class in the community from any share in legislation? I answer, By no means.

They would be factious, discontented, and constantly disturbing the government. It would also be unjust. They have their liberties to protect, as well as others, and the largest share of property. But my idea is, that the Constitution should be so framed as to admit this class, together with a sufficient number of the middling class to control them. You will then combine the abilities and honesty of the community, a proper degree of information, and a disposition to pursue the public good. A representative body, composed principally of respectable yeomanry, is the best possible security to liberty. When the interest of this part of the community is pursued, the public good is pursued, because the body of every nation consists of this class, and because the interest of both the rich and the poor are involved in that of the middling class. No burden can be laid on the poor but what will sensibly affect the middling class. Any law rendering property insecure would be injurious to them. When, therefore, this class in society pursue their own interest, they promote that of the public, for it is involved in it.

In so small a number of representatives, there is great danger from corruption and combination. A great politician has said that every man has his price. I hope this is not true in all its extent; but I ask the gentleman to inform me what government there is in which it has not been practised. Notwithstanding all that has been said of the defects in the constitution of the ancient confederacies in the Grecian republics, their destruction is to be imputed more to this cause than to any imperfection in their forms of government. This was the deadly poison that effected their dissolution. This is an extensive country, increasing in population and growing in consequence. Very many lucrative offices will be in the grant of the government, which will be objects of avarice and ambition. How easy will it be to gain over a sufficient number, in the bestowment of offices, to promote the views and the purposes of those who grant them! Foreign corruption is also to be guarded against. A system of corruption is known to be the system of government in Europe. It is practised without blushing; and we may lay it to our account, it will be attempted amongst us. The most effectual as well as natural security against this is a strong democratic branch in the legislature, frequently chosen, including in it a number of the substantial, sensible yeomanry of the country. Does the House of Representatives answer this description? I confess, to me they hardly wear the complexion of a democratic branch; they appear the mere shadow of representation. The whole number, in both houses, amounts to ninety-one; of these forty-six make a quorum; and twenty-four of those, being secured, may carry any point. Can the liberties of three millions of people be securely trusted in the hands of twenty-four men? Is it prudent to commit to so small a number the decision of the great questions which will come before them? Reason revolts at the idea.

PRO-CONSTITUTIONALISTS

30 FROM *Alexander Hamilton The Federalist Papers, No. 35*

The idea of an actual representation of all classes of the people, by persons of each class, is altogether visionary. Unless it were expressly provided in the Constitution, that each different occupation should send one or more members, the thing would never take place in practice. Mechanics and manufacturers will always be inclined, with few exceptions, to give their votes to merchants, in preference to persons of their own professions or trades. Those discerning citizens are well aware that the mechanic and manufacturing arts furnish the materials of mercantile enterprise and industry. Many of them, indeed, are immediately connected with the operations of commerce. They know that the merchant is their natural patron and friend; and they are aware, that however great the confidence they may justly feel in their own good sense, their interests can be more effectually promoted by the merchant than by themselves. They are sensible that their habits in life have not been such as to give them those acquired endowments,

SOURCE: Alexander Hamilton, *The Federalist Papers,* No. 35, pp. 213–216 (New York: Random House, Inc., Modern Library Edition, 1941).

without which, in a deliberative assembly, the greatest natural abilities are for the most part useless; and that the influence and weight, and superior acquirements of the merchants render them more equal to a contest with any spirit which might happen to infuse itself into the public councils, unfriendly to the manufacturing and trading interests. These considerations, and many others that might be mentioned, prove, and experience confirms it, that artisans and manufacturers will commonly be disposed to bestow their votes upon merchants and those whom they recommend. We must therefore consider merchants as the natural representatives of all these classes of the community.

With regard to the learned professions, little need be observed; they truly form no distinct interest in society, and according to their situation and talents, will be indiscriminately the objects of the confidence and choice of each other, and of other parts of the community.

Nothing remains but the landed interest; and this, in a political view, and particularly in relation to taxes, I take to be perfectly united, from the wealthiest landlord down to the poorest tenant. No tax can be laid on land which will not affect the proprietor of millions of acres as well as the proprietor of a single acre. Every landholder will therefore have a common interest to keep the taxes on land as low as possible; and common interest may always be reckoned upon as the surest bond of sympathy. But if we even could suppose a distinction of interest between the opulent landholder and the middling farmer, what reason is there to conclude, that the first would stand a better chance of being deputed to the national legislature than the last? If we take fact as our guide, and look into our own senate and assembly, we shall find that moderate proprietors of land prevail in both; nor is this less the case in the senate, which consists of a smaller number, than in the assembly, which is composed of a greater number. Where the qualifications of the electors are the same, whether they have to choose a small or a large number, their votes will fall upon those in whom they have most confidence; whether these happen to be men of large fortunes, or of moderate property, or of no property at all.

It is said to be necessary, that all classes of citizens should have some of their own number in the representative body, in order that their feelings and interests may be the better understood and attended to. But we have seen that this will never happen under any arrangement that leaves the votes of the people free. Where this is the case, the representative body, with too few exceptions to have any influence on the spirit of the government, will be composed of landholders, merchants, and men of the learned professions. But where is the danger that the interests and feelings of the different classes of citizens will not be understood or attended to by these three descriptions of men? Will not the landholder know and feel whatever will promote or insure the interest of landed property? And will he not, from his own interest in that species of property, be sufficiently prone to resist every attempt to prejudice or encumber it? Will not the merchant understand and be disposed to cultivate, as far as may be proper, the interests of the mechanic and manufacturing arts, to which his commerce is so nearly allied? Will not the man of the learned profession, who will feel a neutrality to the rivalships between the different branches of industry, be likely to prove an impartial arbiter between them, ready to promote either, so far as it shall appear to him conducive to the general interests of the society?

If we take into the account the momentary humors or dispositions which may happen to prevail in particular parts of the society, and to which a wise administration will never be inattentive, is the man whose situation leads to extensive inquiry and information less likely to be a competent judge of their nature, extent, and foundation than one whose observation does not travel beyond the circle of his neighbors and acquaintances? Is it not natural that a man who is a candidate for the favor of the people, and who is dependent on the suffrages of his fellow-citizens for the continuance of his public honors, should take care to inform himself of their dispositions and inclinations, and should be willing to allow them their proper degree of influence upon his conduct? This dependence, and the necessity of being bound himself, and his posterity, by the laws to which he gives his assent, are the true, and they are the strong chords of sympathy between the representative and the constituent.

There is no part of the administration of government that requires extensive information and a thorough knowledge of the principles of political economy, so much as the business of taxation. The man who understands those principles best will be least likely to resort to oppressive expedients, or to sacrifice any particular class of citizens to the procurement of revenue. It might be demonstrated that the most productive system of finance will always be the least burdensome. There can be no doubt that in order to a judicious exercise of the power of taxation, it is necessary that the person in whose hands it is should be acquainted with the general genius, habits, and modes of thinking of the people at large, and with the resources of the country. And this is all that can be reasonably meant by a knowledge of the interests and feelings of the people. In any other sense the proposition has either no meaning, or an absurd one. And in that sense let every considerate citizen judge for himself where the requisite qualification is most likely to be found.

31 FROM *James Madison*
The Federalist Papers, No. 56

The Second charge against the House of Representatives is, that it will be too small to possess a due knowledge of the interests of its constituents.

As this objection evidently proceeds from a comparison of the proposed number of representatives with the great extent of the United States, the number of their inhabitants, and the diversity of their interests, without taking into view at the same time the circumstances which will distinguish the Congress from other legislative bodies, the best answer that can be given to it will be a brief explanation of these peculiarities.

It is a sound and important principle that the representative ought to be acquainted with the interests and circumstances of his constituents. But this principle can extend no further than to those circumstances and interests to which the authority and care

SOURCE: James Madison in *The Federalist Papers*, No. 56, pp. 365–367 (New York: Random House, Inc., Modern Library Edition, 1941).

of the representative relate. An ignorance of a variety of minute and particular objects, which do not lie within the compass of legislation, is consistent with every attribute necessary to a due performance of the legislative trust. In determining the extent of information required in the exercise of a particular authority, recourse then must be had to the objects within the purview of that authority.

What are to be the objects of federal legislation? Those which are of most importance, and which seem most to require local knowledge, are commerce, taxation, and the militia.

A proper regulation of commerce requires much information, as has been elsewhere remarked; but as far as this information relates to the laws and local situation of each individual State, a very few representatives would be very sufficient vehicles of it to the federal councils.

Taxation will consist, in a great measure, of duties which will be involved in the regulation of commerce. So far the preceding remark is applicable to this object. As far as it may consist of internal collections, a more diffusive knowledge of the circumstances of the State may be necessary. But will not this also be possessed in sufficient degree by a very few intelligent men, diffusively elected within the State? Divide the largest State into ten or twelve districts, and it will be found that there will be no peculiar local interests in either, which will not be within the knowledge of the representative of the district. Besides this source of information, the laws of the State, framed by representatives from every part of it, will be almost of themselves a sufficient guide. In every State there have been made, and must continue to be made, regulations on this subject which will, in many cases, leave little more to be done by the federal legislature, than to review the different laws, and reduce them in one general act. A skilful individual in his closet, with all the local codes before him, might compile a law on some subjects of taxation for the whole Union, without any aid from oral information, and it may be expected that whenever internal taxes may be necessary, and particularly in cases requiring uniformity throughout the States, the more simple objects will be preferred. To be fully sensible of the facility which will be given to this branch of federal legislation by the assistance of the State codes, we need only suppose for a moment that this or any other State were divided into a number of parts, each having and exercising within itself a power of local legislation. Is it not evident that a degree of local information and preparatory labor would be found in the several volumes of their proceedings, which would very much shorten the labors of the general legislature, and render a much smaller number of members sufficient for it?

The federal councils will derive great advantage from another circumstance. The representatives of each State will not only bring with them a considerable knowledge of its laws, and a local knowledge of their respective districts, but will probably in all cases have been members, and may even at the very time be members, of the State legislature, where all the local information and interests of the State are assembled, and from whence they may easily be conveyed by a very few hands into the legislature of the United States.

32 FROM *James Madison*
The Federalist Papers, No. 53

I shall here, perhaps, be reminded of a current observation, "that where annual elections end, tyranny begins." If it be true, as has often been remarked, that sayings which become proverbial are generally founded in reason, it is not less true, that when once established, they are often applied to cases to which the reason of them does not extend. I need not look for a proof beyond the case before us. What is the reason on which this proverbial observation is founded? No man will subject himself to the ridicule of pretending that any natural connection subsists between the sun or the seasons, and the period within which human virtue can bear the temptations of power. Happily for mankind, liberty is not, in this respect, confined to any single point of time; but

SOURCE: James Madison in *The Federalist Papers*, No. 53, pp. 347–351 (New York: Random House, Inc., Modern Library Edition, 1941).

lies within extremes, which afford sufficient latitude for all the variations which may be required by the various situations and circumstances of civil society. The election of magistrates might be, if it were found expedient, as in some instances it actually has been, daily, weekly, or monthly, as well as annual; and if circumstances may require a deviation from the rule on one side, why not also on the other side? Turning our attention to the periods established among ourselves, for the election of the most numerous branches of the State legislatures, we find them by no means coinciding any more in this instance, than in the elections of other civil magistrates. In Connecticut and Rhode Island, the periods are half-yearly. In the other States, South Carolina excepted, they are annual. In South Carolina they are biennial—as is proposed in the federal government. . . .

In searching for the grounds of this doctrine, I can discover but one, and that is wholly inapplicable to our case. The important distinction so well understood in America, between a Constitution established by the people and unalterable by the government, and a law established by the government and alterable by the government, seems to have been little understood and less observed in any other country. Wherever the supreme power of legislation has resided, has been supposed to reside also a full power to change the form of the government. Even in Great Britain, where the principles of political and civil liberty have been most discussed, and where we hear most of the rights of the Constitution, it is maintained that the authority of the Parliament is transcendent and uncontrollable, as well with regard to the Constitution, as the ordinary objects of legislative provision. They have accordingly, in several instances, actually changed, by legislative acts, some of the most fundamental articles of the government. They have in particular, on several occasions, changed the period of election; and, on the last occasion, not only introduced septennial in place of triennial elections, but by the same act, continued themselves in place four years beyond the term for which they were elected by the people. An attention to these dangerous practices has produced a very natural alarm in the votaries of free government, of which frequency of elections is the cornerstone; and has led them to seek for some security to liberty, against the danger to which it is exposed. Where no Constitution, paramount to the government, either existed or could be obtained, no constitutional security, similar to that established in the United States, was to be attempted. Some other security, therefore, was to be sought for; and what better security would the case admit, than that of selecting and appealing to some simple and familiar portion of time, as a standard for measuring the danger of innovations, for fixing the national sentiment, and for uniting the patriotic exertions? The most simple and familiar portion of time, applicable to the subject, was that of a year; and hence the doctrine has been inculcated by a laudable zeal, to erect some barrier against the gradual innovations of an unlimited government, that the advance towards tyranny was to be calculated by the distance of departure from the fixed point of annual elections. But what necessity can there be of applying this expedient to a government limited, as the federal government will be, by the authority of a paramount Constitution? Or who will pretend that the liberties of the people of America will not be more secure under biennial elections, unalterably fixed by such a Constitution, than those of any other nation would be, where elections were annual, or even more frequent, but subject to alterations by the ordinary power of the government?

The second question stated is, whether biennial elections be necessary or useful. The propriety of answering this question in the affirmative will appear from several very obvious considerations.

No man can be a competent legislator who does not add to an upright intention and a sound judgment a certain degree of knowledge of the subjects on which he is to legislate. A part of this knowledge may be acquired by means of information which lie within the compass of men in private as well as public stations. Another part can only be attained, or at least thoroughly attained, by actual experience in the station which requires the use of it. The period of service, ought, therefore, in all such cases, to bear some proportion to the extent of practical knowledge requisite to the due performance of the service. The period of legislative service established in most of the States for the more numerous branch is, as we have seen, one year. The question then may be put into this simple form: does the period of two years bear no greater proportion to the knowledge requisite for federal legisla-

tion than one year does to the knowledge requisite for State legislation? The very statement of the question, in this form, suggests
the answer that ought to be given to it.

In a single State, the requisite knowledge relates to the existing
laws, which are uniform throughout the State, and with which
all the citizens are more or less conversant; and so the general
affairs of the State, which lie within a small compass, are not very
diversified, and occupy much of the attention and conversation of
every class of people. The great theatre of the United States
presents a very different scene. The laws are so far from being
uniform, that they vary in every State; whilst the public affairs of
the Union are spread throughout a very extensive region, and are
extremely diversified by the local affairs connected with them, and
can with difficulty be correctly learnt in any other place than in
the central councils, to which a knowledge of them will be brought
by the representatives of every part of the empire. Yet some
knowledge of the affairs, and even of the laws, of all the States,
ought to be possessed by the members from each of the States.
How can foreign trade be properly regulated by uniform laws,
without some acquaintance with the commerce, the ports, the
usages, and the regulations of the different States? How can the
trade between the different States be duly regulated without some
knowledge of their relative situations in these and other respects?
How can taxes be judiciously imposed and effectually collected,
if they be not accommodated to the different laws and local
circumstances relating to these objects in the different States? How
can uniform regulations for the militia be duly provided, without
a similar knowledge of many internal circumstances by which the
States are distinguished from each other? These are the principal
objects of federal legislation, and suggest most forcibly the extensive information which the representatives ought to acquire.
The other interior objects will require a proportional degree of
information with regard to them.

It is true that all these difficulties will, by degrees, be very much
diminished. The most laborious task will be the proper inaugu-
ration of the government and the primeval formation of a federal
code. Improvements on the first draughts will every year become
both easier and fewer. Past transactions of the government will
be a ready and accurate source of information to new members.

The affairs of the Union will become more and more objects of curiosity and conversation among the citizens at large. And the increased intercourse among those of different States will contribute not a little to diffuse a mutual knowledge of their affairs, as this again will contribute to a general assimilation of their manners and laws. But with all these abatements, the business of federal legislation must continue so far to exceed, both in novelty and difficulty, the legislative business of a single State, as to justify the longer period of service assigned to those who are to transact it.

THE SEPARATION OF POWERS

Both sides in the debate agreed that a constitution must balance power against power so that no element in the system acquired excessive influence. The principal means by which the state constitutions achieved balanced government was to limit the authority of the executive, legislative, and judicial branches. Since the revolutionary generation took a dim view of human nature and believed that men were greedy for power and that power corrupted rulers and threatened liberty, the greatest care and skill were necessary to contrive effective barriers against arbitrary authority. On this score, the anti-Constitutionalists, who had even less faith in their fellow man than did their opponents, found the Constitution dangerously unsatisfactory. The pro-Constitutionalists replied that the framers had scrupulously designed balanced government.

ANTI-CONSTITUTIONALISTS

33 FROM *The Pennsylvania Minority*
The Address and Reasons of Dissent of the Minority of the State of Pennsylvania to Their Constituents

The next consideration that the constitution presents, is the undue and dangerous mixture of the powers of government; the same body possessing legislative, executive and judicial powers. The Senate is a constituent branch of the legislature, it has judicial power in judging on impeachments, and in this case unites in some measure the characters of judge and party, as all the

SOURCE: "The Address and Reasons of Dissent of the Minority of the State of Pennsylvania to their Constituents," in John B. McMaster and Frederick D. Stone, Eds., *Pennsylvania and the Federal Constitution*, pp. 475–477 (Philadelphia: Historical Society of Pennsylvania, 1888).

principal officers are appointed by the president-general, with the concurrence of the Senate, and therefore they derive their offices in part from the Senate. This may bias the judgments of the senators, and tend to screen great delinquents from punishment. And the Senate has, moreover, various and great executive powers, viz., in concurrence with the president-general, they form treaties with foreign nations, that may control and abrogate the constitutions and laws of the several States. Indeed there is no power, privilege or liberty of the State governments, or of the people, but what may be affected by virtue of this power. For all treaties, made by them, are to be the "supreme law of the land; anything in the constitution or laws of any State, to the contrary notwithstanding."

And this great power may be exercised by the President and ten senators (being two-thirds of fourteen, which is a quorum of that body). What an inducement would this offer to the ministers of foreign powers to compass by bribery *such concessions* as could not otherwise be obtained. It is the unvaried usage of all free States, whenever treaties interfere with the positive laws of the land, to make the intervention of the legislature necessary to give them operation. This became necessary, and was afforded by the parliament of Great Britain, in consequence of the late commercial treaty between that kingdom and France. As the Senate judges on impeachments, who is to try the members of the Senate for the abuse of this power! And none of the great appointments to office can be made without the consent of the Senate.

Such various, extensive, and important powers combined in one body of men, are inconsistent with all freedom; the celebrated Montesquieu tells us, that "when the legislative and executive powers are united in the same person, or in the same body of magistrates, there can be no liberty, because apprehensions may arise, lest the same monarch or *senate* should enact tyrannical laws, to execute them in a tyrannical manner."

"Again, there is no liberty, if the power of judging be not separated from the legislative and executive powers. Were it joined with the legislative, the life and liberty of the subject would be exposed to arbitrary control; for the judge would then be legislator. Were it joined to the executive power, the judge might behave with all the violence of an oppressor. There would be an end of everything, were the same man, or the same body of the nobles, or of the people, to exercise those three powers; that of enacting laws, that of executing the public resolutions, and that of judging the crimes or differences of individuals."

The president general is dangerously connected with the senate; his coincidence with the views of the ruling junto in that body, is made essential to his weight and importance in the government, which will destroy all independency and purity in the executive department; and having the power of pardoning without the concurrence of a council, he may screen from punishment the most treasonable attempts that may be made on the liberties of the people, when instigated by his coadjutors in the senate. Instead of this dangerous and improper mixture of the executive with the legislative and judicial, the supreme executive powers ought to have been placed in the president, with a small independent council, made personally responsible for every appointment to office or other act, by having their opinions recorded; and that without the concurrence of the majority of the quorum of this council, the president should not be capable of taking any step.

PRO-CONSTITUTIONALISTS

34 FROM   *James Madison*
The Federalist Papers, No. 47

One of the principal objections inculcated by the more respectable adversaries to the Constitution, is its supposed violation of the political maxim, that the legislative, executive, and judiciary departments ought to be separate and distinct. In the structure of the federal government, no regard, it is said, seems to have been paid to this essential precaution in favor of liberty. The several departments of power are distributed and blended in such a

SOURCE: James Madison in *The Federalist Papers*, No. 47, pp. 312–313 (New York: Random House, Inc., Modern Library Edition, 1941).

manner as at once to destroy all symmetry and beauty of form, and to expose some of the essential parts of the edifice to the danger of being crushed by the disproportionate weight of other parts.

No political truth is certainly of greater intrinsic value, or is stamped with the authority of more enlightened patrons of liberty, than that on which the objection is founded. The accumulation of all powers, legislative, executive, and judiciary, in the same hands, whether of one, a few, or many, and whether hereditary, self-appointed, or elective, may justly be pronounced the very definition of tyranny. Were the federal Constitution, therefore, really chargeable with the accumulation of power, or with a mixture of powers, having a dangerous tendency to such an accumulation, no further arguments would be necessary to inspire a universal reprobation of the system. I persuade myself, however, that it will be made apparent to every one, that the charge cannot be supported, and that the maxim on which it relies has been totally misconceived and misapplied. In order to form correct ideas on this important subject, it will be proper to investigate the sense in which the preservation of liberty requires that the three great departments of power should be separate and distinct.

35 FROM   *James Madison*
The Federalist Papers, No. 51

To what expedient, then, shall we finally resort, for maintaining in practice the necessary partition of power among the several departments, as laid down in the Constitution? The only answer that can be given is, that as all these exterior provisions are found to be inadequate, the defect must be supplied, by so contriving the interior structure of the government as that its

SOURCE: James Madison in *The Federalist Papers,* No. 51. pp. 335–341 (New York: Random House, Inc., Modern Library Edition, 1941).

several constituent parts may, by their mutual relations, be the means of keeping each other in their proper places. Without presuming to undertake a full development of this important idea, I will hazard a few general observations, which may perhaps place it in a clearer light, and enable us to form a more correct judgment of the principles and structure of the government planned by the convention.

But the great security against a gradual concentration of the several powers in the same department, consists in giving to those who administer each department the necessary constitutional means and personal motives to resist encroachments of the others. The provision for defence must in this, as in all other cases, be made commensurate to the danger of attack. Ambition must be made to counteract ambition. The interest of the man must be connected with the constitutional rights of the place. It may be a reflection on human nature, that such devices should be necessary to control the abuses of government. But what is government itself, but the greatest of all reflections on human nature? If men were angels, no government would be necessary. If angels were to govern men, neither external nor internal controls on government would be necessary. In framing a government which is to be administered by men over men, the great difficulty lies in this: you must first enable the government to control the governed; and in the next place oblige it to control itself. A dependence on the people is, no doubt, the primary control on the government; but experience has taught mankind the necessity of auxiliary precautions.

This policy of supplying, by opposite and rival interests, the defect of better motives, might be traced through the whole system of human affairs, private as well as public. We see it particularly displayed in all the subordinate distributions of power, where the constant aim is to divide and arrange the several offices in such a manner as that each may be a check on the other—that the private interest of every individual may be a sentinel over the public rights. These inventions of prudence cannot be less requisite in the distribution of the supreme powers of the State.

But it is not possible to give each department an equal power of self-defence. In republican government, the legislative authority necessarily predominates. The remedy for this inconveniency is to divide the legislature into different branches; and to render them, by different modes of election and different principles of action, as little connected with each other as the nature of their common functions and their common dependence on the society will admit. It may even be necessary to guard against dangerous encroachments by still further precautions. As the weight of the legislative authority requires that it should be thus divided, the weakness of the executive may require, on the other hand, that it should be fortified. An absolute negative on the legislature appears, at first view, to be the natural defence with which the executive magistrate should be armed. But perhaps it would be neither altogether safe nor alone sufficient. On ordinary occasions it might not be exerted with the requisite firmness, and on extraordinary occasions it might be perfidiously abused. May not this defect of an absolute negative be supplied by some qualified connection between this weaker department and the weaker branch of the stronger department, by which the latter may be led to support the constitutional rights of the former, without being too much detached from the rights of its own department?

If the principles on which these observations are founded be just, as I persuade myself they are, and they be applied as a criterion to the several State constitutions, and to the federal Constitution, it will be found that if the latter does not perfectly correspond with them, the former are infinitely less able to bear such a test.

There are, moreover, two considerations particularly applicable to the federal system of America, which place that system in a very interesting point of view.

First. In a single republic, all the power surrendered by the people is submitted to the administration of a single government; and the usurpations are guarded against by a division of the government into distinct and separate departments. In the compound republic of America, the power surrendered by the people is first divided between two distinct governments, and then the portion allotted to each subdivided among distinct and separate departments. Hence a double security arises to the rights of the people. The different governments will control each other, at the same time that each will be controlled by itself.

Second. It is of great importance in a republic not only to guard the society against the oppression of its rulers, but to guard one part of the society against the injustice of the other part. Different interests necessarily exist in different classes of citizens. If a majority be united by a common interest, the rights of the minority will be insecure. There are but two methods of providing against this evil: the one by creating a will in the community independent of the majority—that is, of the society itself; the other, by comprehending in the society so many separate descriptions of citizens as will render an unjust combination of a majority of the whole very improbable, if not impracticable. The first method prevails in all governments possessing an hereditary or self-appointed authority. This, at best, is but a precarious security; because a power independent of the society may as well espouse the unjust views of the major, as the rightful interests of the minor party, and may possibly be turned against both parties. The second method will be exemplified in the federal republic of the United States. Whilst all authority in it will be derived from and dependent on the society, the society itself will be broken into so many parts, interests and classes of citizens, that the rights of individuals, or of the minority, will be in little danger from interested combinations of the majority. In a free government the security for civil rights must be the same as that for religious rights. It consists in the one case in the multiplicity of interests, and in the other in the multiplicity of sects. The degree of security in both cases will depend on the number of interests and sects; and this may be presumed to depend on the extent of country and number of people comprehended under the same government. This view of the subject must particularly recommend a proper federal system to all the sincere and considerate friends of republican government, since it shows that in exact proportion as the territory of the Union may be formed into more circumscribed Confederacies, or States, oppressive combinations of a majority will be facilitated; the best security, under the republican forms, for the rights of every class of citizens, will be diminished; and consequently the stability and independence of some member of the government, the only other security, must be proportionally increased. Justice is the end of government.

It is the end of civil society. It ever has been and ever will be pursued until it be obtained, or until liberty be lost in the pursuit. In a society under the forms of which the stronger faction can readily unite and oppress the weaker, anarchy may as truly be said to reign as in a state of nature, where the weaker individual is not secured against the violence of the stronger; and as, in the latter state, even the stronger individuals are prompted, by the uncertainty of their condition, to submit to a government which may protect the weak as well as themselves; so, in the former state, will the more powerful factions or parties be gradually induced, by a like motive, to wish for a government which will protect all parties, the weaker as well as the more powerful. It can be little doubted that if the State of Rhode Island was separated from the Confederacy and left to itself, the insecurity of rights under the popular form of government within such narrow limits would be displayed by such reiterated oppressions of factious majorities that some power altogether independent of the people would soon be called for by the voice of the very factions whose misrule had proved the necessity of it. In the extended republic of the United States, and among the great variety of interests, parties, and sects which it embraces, a coalition of a majority of the whole society could seldom take place on any other principles than those of justice and the general good; whilst there being thus less danger to a minor from the will of a major party, there must be less pretext, also, to provide for the security of the former, by introducing into the government a will not dependent on the latter, or, in other words, a will independent of the society itself. It is no less certain than it is important, notwithstanding the contrary opinions which have been entertained, that the larger the society, provided it lie within a practical sphere, the more duly capable it will be of self-government. And happily for the *republican cause,* the practicable sphere may be carried to a very great extent, by a judicious modification and mixture of the *federal principle.*

PART SIX

The Legacy of the Founding Fathers

The founding fathers were not democrats. As students of history, familiar with the failures of democratic government in antiquity and from their own experience, skeptical of relying exclusively on majorities to govern wisely and well, they were even more opposed to placing power in the hands of kings and aristocrats. The Federal Constitution, as Douglas Adair argues in the following essay, attempted to escape from this dilemma. The founding fathers acknowledged the people as the ultimate source of power and gave them direct choice of representatives to Congress but they left the selection of the president, the senate, and the judiciary to the elected representatives of the people. They assumed that citizens would defer to the wisdom, experience, and virtue of upper class leaders yet at the same time they made American elites theoretically, if not practically, dependent on popular approval. Deference, however, declined in the first half century following the American Revolution, as the result of chronic conflict within the elite and between those on top and ambitious newcomers pushing their way forward and appealing to the principles of popular rule. The Constitution was thus transformed into an instrument of democratic government, something not quite intended by the framers. Similarly the framers gave anxious Southerners written guarantees that the Union would not jeopardize the institution of slavery, though most Northerners opposed it. This compromise gained the framers necessary support in the South but in the long run the creation of a powerful Union in which anti-slavery sentiment flourished after 1830 helped to break the chains that bound the black man.

167

Often celebrated for their realism and political shrewdness, the founding fathers were also dreamers, infected with the belief that the mission of America was to demonstrate at last the practicality of government based on the consent of the governed. "In this way," James Madison intoned, "the citizens of the United States are responsible for the greatest trust ever confided to a political authority."

36 FROM   *Douglass G. Adair*
"Experience Must be Our Only Guide:" History, *Democratic Theory, and the United States Constitution*

"The history of Greece," John Adams wrote in 1786, "should be to our countrymen what is called in many families on the Continent, a *boudoir,* an octagonal apartment in a house, with a full-length mirror on every side, and another in the ceiling. The use of it is, when any of the young ladies, or young gentlemen if you will, are at any time a little out of humour, they may retire to a place where, in whatever direction they turn their eyes, they see their own faces and figures multiplied without end. By thus beholding their own beautiful persons, and seeing, at the same time, the deformity brought upon them by their anger, they may recover their tempers and their charms together."

Adams' injunction that his countrymen should study the history of ancient Greece in order to amend their political behavior suggests two points for our consideration. First, John Adams assumed without question that history did offer lessons and precepts which statesmen could use in solving immediate problems. Secondly, Adams urged the study of the classical Greek republics as the particular history especially relevant, most full of useful lessons and precepts for Americans in 1787.

Adams, as is well known, practiced what he preached. Working at high speed between October 1786 and January 1787, in time stolen from his duties as United States Minister to Great Britain, he composed his *Defence of the Constitutions of the United States*—a 300-page book exhibiting for his countrymen the lessons of history. And though he included material from all periods of western civilization, a large part of his data was collected from

SOURCE: Douglass G. Adair, " 'Experience Must be Our Only Guide:' History, Democratic Theory, and the United States Constitution," in Ray A. Billington, Ed., *The Reinterpretation of Early American History*, pp. 129–144 (San Marino: Huntington Library, 1966). Reprinted by permission of the publisher and the editor.

the classical republics of antiquity.

Nor did his American audience who read Adams' work in the weeks immediately prior to the meeting of the Philadelphia Convention deny his assumptions or purposes in urging them to study the lessons of Greek history. Benjamin Rush, for example, reporting to the Reverend Richard Price in England on the attitude of the Pennsylvania delegation to the Convention, gave Adams' study the highest praise. "Mr. Adams' book," he wrote, "has diffused such excellent principles among us that there is little doubt of our adopting a vigorous and compounded federal legislature. Our illustrious Minister in this gift to his country has done us more service than if he had obtained alliances for us with all the nations of Europe."

Do Adams and Rush in their view on the utility of history for the constitutional reforms of 1787 represent the typical attitude of the members of the Convention? Did the fifty-five men gathered to create a more perfect union consciously turn to past history for lessons and precepts that were generalized into theories about the correct organization of the new government? Did lessons from the antique past, applied to their present situation, concretely affect their actions at Philadelphia? The evidence is overwhelming that they did, although the weight of modern commentary on the Constitution either ignores the Fathers' conscious and deliberate use of history and theory or denies that it played any important part in their deliberations.

Max Farrand, for example, after years of study of the debates in the Convention concluded that the members were anything but historically oriented. Almost all had served (Farrand noted) in the Continental Congress and had tried to govern under the impotent Articles of Confederation. There is little of importance in the Constitution (Farrand felt) that did not arise from the effort to correct specific defects of the Confederation.

Robert L. Schuyler, an able and careful student of the Constitution, goes even further in denying the Convention's dependence upon history. "The Fathers were practical men. They lived at a time when a decent respect for the proprieties of political discussion required at least occasional reference to Locke and Montesquieu . . . but . . . such excursions into political philosophy as were made are to be regarded rather as purple patches than as integral parts of the proceedings. The scholarly Madison had gone extensively into the subject of Greek federalism ... but it was his experience in public life and his wide knowledge of the conditions of his day, not his classical lucubrations that bore fruit at Philadelphia.... The debate ... did not proceed along theoretical lines. John Dickinson expressed the prevailing point of view when he said in the Convention: 'Experience must be our only guide. Reason may mislead us.' "

Dickinson's statement on August 13th: "Experience must be our only guide" does indeed express the mood of the delegates; no word was used more often; time after time "experience" was appealed to as the clinching argument for a controverted opinion. But "experience" as used in the Convention, more often than not, referred to the precepts of history. This is Dickinson's sense of the word when he warned the Convention that "reason" might mislead. "It was not reason," Dickinson continued, "that discovered the singular and admirable mechanism of the English Constitution ... [or the] mode of trial by jury. Accidents probably produced these discoveries, and experience has given a sanction to them." And then Dickinson, turning to James Wilson and Madison who had argued that vesting the power to initiate revenue bills exclusively in the lower house of the Legislature had proved "pregnant with altercation in every [American] State where the [revolutionary] Constitution had established it," denied that the short "experience" of the American States carried as weighty a sanction as the long historic "experience" of the English House of Commons. "Shall we oppose to this long [English] experience," Dickinson asked, "the short experience of 11 years which we had ourselves, on this subject." Dickinson's words actually point to the fact that theories grounded in historical research are indeed integral parts of the debate on the Constitution.

For Dickinson is not alone in using "experience" in this dual fashion to refer both to political wisdom gained by participation in events, and wisdom gained by studying past events. Franklin and Madison, Butler and Mason, Wilson and Hamilton all appeal to historical "experience" in exactly the same way. "Experience shows" or "history proves" are expressions that are used interchangeably throughout the Convention by members from all sections of the United States. Pure reason not verified by history might be a false guide; the mass of mankind might indeed be the slave of passion and unreason, but the fifty-five men who gathered at Philadelphia in 1787 labored in the faith of the enlightenment that experience-as-history provided "the least fallible guide of human opinions," that historical experience is "the oracle of truth, and where its responses are unequivocal they ought to be conclusive and sacred."

Schuyler's insistence that the Fathers were "practical men" who abhorred theory, associates him with a standard theme of American anti-intellectualism that honors unsystematic "practicality" and distrusts systematic theoretical thought. His argument, undoubtedly too, reflects nineteenth-century theories of "progress-evolution" that assume the quantitative lapse in time between 400 B.C. and 1787 A.D. *a priori* makes the earlier period irrelevant for understanding a modern and different age. And, of course, what came to be called "sound history" after 1880 when the discipline came to roost in academic groves, is quite different itself from the "history" that eighteenth-century statesmen found most significant and useful. Modern historians have tended to insist that the unique and the particular is the essence of "real history"; in contrast the eighteenth-century historian was most concerned and put the highest value on what was universal and constant through time.

Eighteenth-century historians believed "that there is a great uniformity among the actions of men, in all nations and ages, and that human nature remains still the same, in its principles and operations. The same motives always produce the same actions; the same events follow from the same causes. Ambition, avarice, self-love, vanity, friendship, generosity, public spirit; these passions, mixed in various degrees, and distributed through society, have been from the beginning of the world, and still are the source of all the actions and enterprizes, which have ever been observed among mankind. Would you know the sentiments, inclinations, and course of life of the Greeks and Romans? Study well the temper and actions of the French and English." Thus David Hume, distinguished eighteenth-century historian and philosopher.

The method of eighteenth-century history for those who would gain political wisdom from it followed from this primary assumption—it was historical-comparative synthesis. Again Hume speaks: "Mankind are so much the same, in all times and places, that history informs us of nothing new or strange, in this particular. *Its chief use is only to discover the constant and universal principles of human nature,* by showing men in all varieties of circumstances and situations, and furnishing us with materials, from which we may form our observations and become acquainted with the regular springs of human action and behavior. These records . . . are so many collections of experiments, by which the politician or moral philosopher fixes the principles of his science, in the same manner as the physician or natural philosopher becomes acquainted with the nature of plants, minerals, and other external objects, by the experiments which he forms concerning them."

John Adams would echo Hume's argument and use the identical metaphor in the preface to his *Defence.* "The systems of legislators are experiments made on human life, and manners, society and government. Zoroaster, Confucius, Mithras, Odin, Thor, Mohamet, Lycurgus, Solon, Romulus and a thousand others may be compared to philosophers making experiments on the elements." Adams was too discreet to list his own name with the Great Legislators of the past, but in his own mind, we know from his *Diary* and letters to his wife, he identified himself with Moses, Lycurgus, and Solon as the Lawgiver of his state, Massachusetts, whose republican constitution, based on his study of history, he had written almost single-handed in October 1779. Now eight years later his *Defence* both justified the form of government he had prepared for his own state and "fixed the principles"—to use Hume's words—of the science of government that ought to be followed in modeling a more perfect union of the states. Adams' book, in complete accord with eighteenth-century canons, was a comparative-historical survey of constitutions reaching back to Minos, Lycurgus, and Solon.

History proved, Adams felt sure, "that there can be no free government without a democratical branch in the constitution." But he was equally sure that "Democracy, simple democracy, never had a patron among men of letters." Rousseau, indeed, had argued, as Adams pointed out, that "a society of Gods would govern themselves democratically," but this is really an ironic admission by "the eloquent philosopher of Geneva that it is not practicable to govern *Men* in this way." For very short periods of time pure democracy had existed in antiquity, but "from the frightful pictures of a democratical city, drawn by the masterly pencils of ancient philosophers and historians, it may be conjectured that such governments existed in Greece and Italy... [only] for short spaces of time." Such is the nature of pure democracy, or simple democracy, that this form of government carries in its very constitution, infirmities and vices that doom it to speedy disaster. Adams agreed completely with Jonathan Swift's pronouncement that if the populace of a country actually attempted to rule and establish a government by the people they would soon become their "own dupe, a mere underworker and a purchaser in trust for some single tyrant whose state and power they advance to their own ruin, with as blind an instinct as those worms that die with weaving magnificent habits for beings of a superior order to their own." It was not surprising then to Adams that when he surveyed contemporary Europe he found no functioning democracy. Indeed, governments that had even the slightest "democratical mixture" in their constitutions "are annihilated all over Europe, except on a barren rock, a paltry fen, an inaccessible mountain, or an impenetrable forest." The one great exception outside of the American states where a democratic element was part of the constitution was Britain, the great monarchical or regal republic. And as Adams contemplated the English Constitution, he felt it to be "the most stupendous fabric of human invention.... Not the formation of languages, not the whole art of navigation and shipbuilding does more honor to the human understanding than this system of government."

The problem for Americans in 1787 was to recognize the principles exemplified in Britain, Adams thought, and to frame governments to give the people "a legal, constitutional" *share* in the process of government—it should operate through representation; there should be a balance in the legislature of lower house and upper house; and there should be a total separation of the executive from the legislative power, and of the judicial from both. Above all, if the popular principles of government were to be preserved in America it was necessary to maintain an independent and powerful executive: "If there is one certain truth to be collected from the history of all ages, it is this; that the people's rights and liberties, and the democratical mixture in a constitution, can never be preserved without a strong executive, or, in other words, without separating the executive from the legislative power. If the executive power ... is left in the hands either of an aristocratical or democratical assembly, it will corrupt the legislature as necessarily as rust corrupts iron, or as arsenic poisons the human body; and when the legislature is corrupted, the people are undone."

And then John Adams took on the role of scientific prophet. If Americans learned the lessons that history taught, their properly limited democratic constitutions would last for ages. Only long in the future when "the present states become ... rich, powerful, and luxurious, as well as numerous, [will] their ... good sense ... dictate to them what to do; they may [then] make transitions to a nearer resemblance of the British constitution," and presumably make their first magistrates and their senators hereditary.

But note the ambiguity which underlies Adams' historical thinking. Science, whether political or natural, traditionally has implied determinism—scientific prediction is possible only because what was, is, and ever shall be. Reason thus might be free to discover the fixed pattern of social phenomena, but the phenomena themselves follow a pre-destined course of development. The seventeenth-century reason of Isaac Newton discovered the laws of the solar system, but no man could change those laws or the pattern of the planets' orbits; Karl Marx might in the nineteenth century discover the scientific laws of economic institutions, but no man could reform them or change the pattern in which the feudal economy inevitably degenerated into bourgeois economy, which in its turn worked inexorably toward its predetermined and proletarian end.

In the same fashion Adams' scientific reading of history committed him and his contemporaries in varying degrees of rigidity to a species of *political determinism*. History showed, so they believed, that there were only three basic types of government: monarchy, aristocracy, and democracy, or government of the one, the few, or the many. Moreover history showed, so they believed, that each of these three types when once established had particular and terrible defects—"mortal diseases," Madison was to call these defects—that made each pure type quickly degenerate: Every monarchy tended to degenerate into a tyranny. Every aristocracy, or government of the few, by its very nature, was predestined to evolve into a corrupt and unjust oligarchy. And the democratic form, as past experience proved, inevitably worked toward anarchy, class-conflict, and social disorder of such virulence that it normally ended in dictatorship.

On this deterministic-theory of a uniform and constant human nature, inevitably operating inside a fixed-pattern of limited political forms, producing a predictable series of evil political results, John Adams based his invitation to Americans to study the classical republics. This assumption of determinism explains the constant and reiterated appeal to Greek and Roman "experience," both during the Philadelphia Convention and in the State ratifying conventions. At the beginning of the Revolution Adams had invited his rebellious compatriots to study English history, for from 1765 to 1776 the immediate and pressing questions of practical politics related to the vices and corruption of the English monarchy. But after 1776 at which time Americans committed their political destinies to thirteen democratic frames of government loosely joined in a Confederation, English monarchical history became temporarily less relevant to American problems. The American States of 1776 in gambling on democratic republics stood alone in the political world. Nowhere in contemporary Europe or Asia could Americans turn for reassuring precedents showing functioning republican government. So, increasingly from 1776 to 1787, as Americans learned in practice the difficulties of making republican systems work, the leaders among the Revolutionary generation turned for counsel to classical history. They were *obliged* to study Greece and Rome if they would gain "experimental" wisdom on the dangers and potentialities of the republican form. Only in classical history could they observe the long-range predictable tendencies of those very "vices" of their democratic Confederacy that they were now enduring day by day.

It was these frightening lessons from classical history added to their own present difficulties under the Confederation that produced the total dimension of the crisis of 1787. Standing, as it were, in John Adams' hall of magic mirrors where past and present merged in a succession of terrifying images, the Founding Fathers could not conceal from themselves that Republicanism in America might already be doomed. Was it indeed possible to maintain stable republican government in any of the thirteen American States? And even if some of the States units could maintain republicanism, could union be maintained in a republican confederation?

The answer of history to both of these questions seemed to be an emphatic "no." As Alexander Hamilton reminded the Convention June 18th and later reminded the country speaking as Publius, "It is impossible to read the history of the petty Republics of Greece and Italy without feeling sensations of horror and disgust at the distractions with which they were continually agitated, and at the rapid succession of revolutions, by which they were kept in a state of perpetual vibration between the extremes of tyranny and anarchy. If they exhibit occasional calms, these only serve as short-lived contrasts to the furious storms that are to succeed. If now and then intervals of felicity open themselves to view, we behold them with a mixture of regret, arising from the reflection, that the pleasing scenes before us are soon to be overwhelmed by the tempestuous waves of sedition and party rage."

Hamilton along with Madison, Adams, Jefferson, and every educated eighteenth-century statesman thus knew from history that the mortal disease of democratical republics was and always would be the class struggle that had eventually destroyed every republican state in history. And *now* with the "desperate debtor" Daniel Shays, an American Cataline—an American Alcibiades— proving only ten years after independence, the class struggle was raising monitory death's-heads among the barely united republican States of America. If potential class war was implicit in every republic, so too did war characterize the interstate relations of adjacent republics. The only union that proved adequate to unite Athens and Sparta, Thebes and Corinth in one functioning peaceful whole was the monarchical power of Philip of Macedon; Rome, after conquering her neighbor city states, it is true, had maintained republican liberty for a relatively long period, in spite of internal conflict of plebes and patricians, but when the Empire increased in extent, when her geographical boundaries were enlarged, Roman liberty died and an Emperor displaced the Senate as the center of Roman authority. In 1787 the authority of scholars, philosophers, and statesmen was all but unanimous in arguing (from the experience of history) that no republic ever could be established in a territory as extended as the United States—that even if established for a moment, class war must eventually destroy every democratic republic.

These were the two lessons that Hamilton insisted in his great speech of June 18 the Constitutional Convention must remember. These were the lessons that were stressed in John Adams' morbid anatomy of fifty historic republican constitutions. This was the theme of Madison's arguments (which the Convention accepted) for junking entirely the feeble Articles of the Confederation in favor of a government that would, it was hoped, neutralize interstate conflict and class war. It was because these lessons were accepted by so many educated men in America that the commercial crisis of 1784-5 had become a political crisis by 1786, and a moral crisis by 1787.

Had the Revolution been a mistake from the beginning? Had the blood and treasure of Americans spent in seven years of war against England ironically produced republican systems in which rich and poor New Englanders must engage in bloody class war among themselves? Had independence merely guaranteed a structure in which Virginians and Pennsylvanians would cut each others' throats until one conquered the other or some foreign crown conquered both?

From our perspective, 179 years later, this may appear an hysterical and distorted analysis of the situation of the United States in 1787, but we, of course, are the beneficiaries of the Fathers' practical solution to this problem that *their* reading of history forced upon them. Americans today have the historic experience of living peacefully in the republic stabilized by their Constitution. History has reassured us concerning what only the wisest among them dared to hope in 1787: that the republican form could indeed be adapted to a continental territory. Priestley, a sympathetic friend of the American Revolution was speaking the exact truth in 1791 when he said: "It was taken for granted that the moment America had thrown off the yoke of Great Britain, the different states would go to war among themselves."

When Hamilton presented his analysis of the vices of republicanism to his acceptant audience in Philadelphia, he also offered the traditional remedy which statesmen and philosophers from antiquity on had proposed as the ONLY cure for the evils of the three types of pure government. This remedy was to "mix" or "compound" elements of monarchy, aristocracy, and democracy into one balanced structure. There was, Hamilton reasoned, little danger of class war in a state which had a king vested with more power than the political organs of government representing either the rich or the poor. The "size of the country" and the "amazing turbulence" of American democracy made him despair of republicanism in the United States, without an elective monarch who once in office could not be voted out by majority rule. The people, i.e., the multitudinous poor, would directly elect the lower house of the legislature; a Senate to represent the rich would be elected for life; and to guard against the poison of democracy in the separate States, they would be transformed into administrative districts with their governors appointed by the elected King.

We mistake the significance of Hamilton's proposal of an elective monarch as a solution of the crisis of 1787 if we think of his plan as either *original* or *unrepresentative* of the thought of important segments of American opinion in 1787. The strength of Hamilton's logical position lay in the fact that his proposal was the traditional, the standard, indeed, as history showed the *only* solution for the specific dangers of interclass and interstate conflict that were destroying the imperfect Union. As early as 1776 Carter Braxton had offered almost this identical plan as the ideal constitution for Virginia. In May, 1782, reasoning parallel to Hamilton's had emboldened Colonel Lewis Nicola to invite Washington to use the Army to set himself up as a King. And after Shays' rebellion voices grew louder, particularly in the New England and the Middle States, proposing two cures for the ills of America. One cure was to divide the unwieldy Confederation into two or three small units; the other was the creation of an American throne. We have Washington's word for it that the most alarming feature of this revival of monarchical sentiment was its appearance among staunch "republican characters"—men who like Hamilton had favored independence in 1776 but who had become disillusioned about ever achieving order and security in a republic. Add to this group of new converts the large bloc of old Tories who had never forsaken their allegiance to monarchy, and it is easy to see why Washington, Madison, and other leaders were seriously alarmed that Union would break up and that kings would reappear in the Balkanized segments.

Furthermore, at the very time the Philadelphia Convention was rejecting Hamilton's mixed-monarchy as a present solution for the vices of American democracy, leading members of the Convention most tenacious of republicanism accepted the fact that an American monarchy was inevitable at some future date. As Mr. Williamson of North Carolina remarked, on July 24, "it was pretty certain . . . that we should at some time or other have a king; but he wished no precaution to be omitted that might postpone the event as long as possible." There is a curious statistical study of Madison's which points to his certainty also, along with the precise prophecy that the end of republicanism in the United States would come approximately 142 years after 1787—about the decade of the 1930's. John Adams' *Defence* contains the same sort of prophecy. "In future ages," Adams remarked, "if the present States become great nations, rich, powerful, and luxurious, as well as numerous," the "feelings and good sense" of Americans "will dictate to them" reform of their governments "to a nearer resemblance of the British Constitution," complete with a hereditary king and a hereditary Senate. Gouverneur Morris is reported to have argued during the Convention "we must have a Monarch sooner or later . . . and the sooner we take him while we are able to make a Bargain with him, the better." Nor did the actual functioning of the Constitution during its first decade of existence lighten Morris' pessimism; in 1804 he was arguing that the crisis would come sooner rather than later. Even Franklin, the least doctrinaire of the Fathers—perhaps with Jefferson the most hopeful among the whole Revolutionary generation regarding the potentialities of

American democracy—accepted the long-range pessimism of the Hamiltonian analysis. Sadly the aged philosopher noted, June 2, "There is a natural inclination in mankind to kingly government. . . . I am apprehensive, therefore,—perhaps too apprehensive,— that the government of these States may in future times end in monarchy. But this catastrophe, I think may be long delayed. . . ."

The "precious advantage" that the United States had in 1787 that offered hope for a "republican remedy for the diseases most incident to republican government"—the circumstance which would delay the necessity of accepting Hamilton's favored form of mixed monarchy—lay in the predominance of small free-hold farmers among the American population. Since the time of Aristotle, it had been recognized that yeomen farmers—a middle class between the greedy rich and the envious poor—provided the most stable foundation upon which to erect a popular govern-ment. This factor, commented on by Madison, Pinckney, Adams and others, helps explain why the Convention did not feel it necessary to sacrifice either majority rule or popular responsi-bility in their new Constitution.

Of equal importance was the factor of expedience. Less doctri-naire than Alexander Hamilton, the leaders of the Convention realized that a theoretical best—and member after member went on record praising the British Constitution as *the best* ever created by man—a theoretical best might be the enemy of a possible good. As Pierce Butler insisted, in a different context, "The people will not bear such innovations. . . . Supposing such an establishment to be useful, we must not venture on it. We must follow the example of Solon who gave the Athenians not the best government he could devise, but the best they would receive."

Consequently the Constitution that emerged from the Conven-tion's debates was, as Madison described it a "novelty in the political world"—a "fabric" of government which had "no model on the face of the globe." It was an attempt to approximate in a structure of balanced republican government the advantages of stability that such mixed governments as Great Britain's had derived from hereditary monarchy and a hereditary House of Lords.

It was an "experiment" as members of the Convention frankly

admitted, but one about which most of the Fathers could be hopeful because it adapted to the concrete circumstances of the United States of 1787, the experience of mankind through all ages as revealed by history. Driven by the collapse of the Confederation, the depression of 1785-86, and Shays' Rebellion to take stock of their political situation six years after Yorktown had won for Americans the opportunity for self-government, the Fathers had turned to history, especially classical history, to help them analyze their current difficulties. Their reading of history, equally with their immediate experience, defined for them both the short-range and the long-range potentialities for evil inherent in a uniform human nature operating in a republican government. But their reading of history also suggested a specific type of government that would remedy the evils they already knew and those worse evils they expected to come. Utilizing this knowledge, building on the solid core of agreement which historical wisdom had helped supply, they created, by mutual concession and compromise, a governmental structure as nearly like mixed-government as it was possible to approach while maintaining the republican principle of majority rule. And this they offered the American people *hoping* it would be ratified, *hoping* that after ratification their "experiment" with all its compromises of theory and interest would provide a more perfect union.

If there is substance in the argument offered in the foregoing paragraphs, it should throw some light, at least, on the intellectual confusion exhibited during the last half-century by many learned commentators in discussing the nature of our Constitution. This confused and confusing debate has focused in part on the question: "did the Fathers write a 'democratic' Constitution?" The answers given have been almost as "mixed" as the theory to which the Framers subscribed.

Part of the bother lies in the lack of precision with which the word *democracy* was used then, and the even more unprecise way that we use it now. The more a word is used the less exact its meaning becomes, and in our day *democratic/democracy* has been extended to describe art, foreign policy, literature, etc., etc. Thus, from being a somewhat technical word of political discourse, in 1787, it has become a perfect sponge of squashy vagueness. Luckily, the context of formal theory that mixed government did imply in 1787 does allow us to recognize certain rather concrete and specific features usually associated, then, with the democratic form of government. In the first place, the very concept of "mixture" implies a relativism that modern doctrinaire democrats often forget: a political system, in 1787, was thought of as more-or-less democratic, as possessing few or many democratic features. Only in the pure form was democracy an either/or type of polity. In the second place, the simple democratic form was almost always thought of as appropriate only for a tiny territorial area—Madison in *Federalist 10,* for instance, would only equate the word with the direct democracy of the classical city-state. Thirdly, the functional advantages and disadvantages of the pure democratic form of government were almost universally agreed upon. A government *by* the people (so it was thought) always possessed *fidelity* to the common good; it was impossible for a people not to *desire* and to *intend* to promote the general welfare. However, the vices of democracy were that the people, collectively, were not *wise* about the correct measures to serve this great end and that the people could be easily duped by demagogues, who, flattering their good hearts and muddled heads, would worm their way to unlimited power. It was well-meaning stupidity, the capacity for thoughtless injustice, the fickle instability of the popular will, that led the classical theorists, who the Fathers were familiar with, to designate "pure democracy" as a form doomed to a short existence that tended to eventuate, with a pendulum swing, in the opposite extreme of tyranny and dictatorship.

In dark contrast to this *fidelity* of the democratic many was the vice afflicting both monarchy and aristocracy: an inveterate and incorrigible tendency to use the apparatus of government to serve the special selfish interests of the one or the few. However, the aristocratic form offered, so it was believed, the best possibility of *wisdom,* in planning public measures, while monarchy promised the necessary *energy, secrecy,* and *dispatch* for executing policy.

It is in this ideological context that one can deduce some of the intentions of the authors of our Constitution. It is clear, I think, that the office and power of the President was consciously designed to provide the *energy, secrecy,* and *dispatch* traditionally associated with the monarchical form. Thus Patrick Henry, considering the proposed Chief Executive and recognizing that the President was not unlike an elective king, could cry with reason that the Constitution "squints toward monarchy." But it was equally possible for Richard Henry Lee, focusing on the Senate, to complain that the document had a "strong tendency to aristocracy." This was said by Lee six months before Madison, in *Federalists 62-63,* explicitly defended the Senate as providing the *wisdom* and the *stability*—"aristocratic virtues"—needed to check the fickle lack of wisdom that Madison predicted would characterize the people's branch of the new government, the Lower House. Nor were there other critics lacking who, recognizing that the Constitution ultimately rested on popular consent, who, seeing that despite the ingenious apparatus designed to temper the popular will by introducing into the compound modified monarchical/aristocratic ingredients, could argue that the new Constitution was too democratic to operate effectively as a national government in a country as large and with a population as heterogeneous as the Americans'. One such was William Grayson, who doubted the need of *any* national government, but who felt, if one was to be established, it ought to provide a President and a Senate elected for life terms, these to be balanced by a House of Representatives elected triennially.

It is, thus, significant that if modern scholars are confused and disagreed about the nature of the Constitution today, so, too, in 1787-1788, contemporary observers were also confused and also disagreed as to whether it was monarchical, aristocratic, or democratic in its essence.

My own opinion is that the Constitution of 1787 is probably best described in a term John Adams used in 1806. Writing to Benjamin Rush, September 19, 1806, Adams, disapproving strongly of Jefferson's style as President, bemoaned the fact that Jefferson and his gang had now made the national government "to all intents and purposes, in virtue, spirit, and effect a democracy."—Alas! "I once thought," said Adams, "our Constitution was *quasi* or mixed government,"—but alas!

"Quasi," or better still "quasi-mixed"—for, given the American people's antipathy to monarchy after 1776, and given the non-aristocratic nature (in a European sense) of the American upper class of 1787, the Constitution at best, or worst, could only be "*quasi*-mixed," since there were not "ingredients" available in the United States to compose a genuine mixture in the classic sense. So what the Fathers fashioned was a "quasi-mixed" Constitution that, given the "genius" of the American people, had a strong and inevitable tendency that "squinted" from the very beginning towards the national democracy that would finally develop in the nineteenth century.

SUGGESTIONS FOR FURTHER READING

Nation-Building, American Style

The American constitution was the result of a long, complicated process of nation-building that began with the Declaration of Independence, which formally transformed thirteen colonies into the United States. For at least a generation the new union was in serious danger of foundering as Americans confronted many of the problems other new nations have faced more recently. Although nation-building in the United States was unique, the American experience has been illuminated by recent studies by political scientists and sociologists of the *process* by which nations are created—investigations that have received impetus from the creation of many new nations in Asia and Africa within the last twenty years. An excellent introduction to this literature is Lucian W. Pye's, *The Crises in Political Development* (Boston, 1966),* which summarizes and synthesizes a good deal of scholarship. The essays in Joseph La Palombara and Myron Weiner, Eds., *Political Parties and Political Development* (Princeton, 1961) focus on the role of political parties in nation-building, with a chapter by William N. Chambers examining the American experience in the late eighteenth century. Seymour M. Lipset, *The First New Nation* (New York, 1963),* applies a developmental analysis to the American case in a more general way. Historians have just begun to exploit the insights of this new approach but two traditional works are especially valuable: Edmund S. Morgan, *The Birth of the Republic, 1763–1789* (Chicago, 1956) * is the best modern survey of the revolutionary era and Robert R. Palmer, *The Age of the Democratic Revolution: The Challenge* (Princeton, 1959),* and the second volume, *The Response* (Princeton, 1964) revealingly place American events in the larger context of revolutionary developments in the Western world.

The American Revolution and the Constitution

The Federal Constitution was the product of theory and experience that reached back into the colonial past and especially to the crisis that

* Available in paper back.

led to the Revolution and the efforts to establish new governments in the states and the nation. Basic to understanding the origins of the Federal Constitution and the purposes of the founding fathers is Bernard Bailyn's *Ideological Origins of the American Revolution* (Cambridge, 1967) which unravels the cardinal political assumptions of the revolutionary movement, including the leadership that later became involved in framing the Federal Constitution. For the colonial roots of revolutionary thought see Bailyn's *Origins of American Politics* (New York, 1968). Gordon Wood in *The Creation of the American Republic* (Chapel Hill, 1969) pursues revolutionary political thinking through the War for Independence and into the 1780s with remarkable insight and originality. And J. R. Pole's *Political Representation in England and the Origins of the American Republic* (New York, 1966) illuminates transformations in the colonial and revolutionary period in English notions of representation, a central problem faced by the Philadelphia Convention. Benjamin Wright's *Consensus and Continuity, 1776–1787* (Boston, 1958) * is a brief, earlier attempt to reassess the constitutional history of the revolutionary period and offers a counterview to the class-conflict interpretation of Charles A. Beard and the progressive historians.

More specialized studies of political developments in the states clarify the origins of the Federal Constitution. Allan Nevins, *The American States During and After the Revolution* (New York, 1924) is a mine of information, state by state, for political developments, without being marred unduly by an inconsistent application of a class-conflict interpretation. See also Elisha P. Douglas, *Rebels and Democrats* (Chapel Hill, 1955).* Of particular value are two documentary collections on Massachusetts where the process of constitution making was unusually complex and generated a great deal of controversy. Oscar and Mary F. Handlin in *The Popular Sources of Political Authority* (Cambridge, 1966) have collected source materials and their introduction is especially enlightening. See also a briefer collection by Robert Taylor, *Massachusetts, Colony to Commonwealth* (Chapel Hill, 1961).* Two other useful studies focusing on the states are J. P. Selsam, *The Pennsylvania Constitution* (Philadelphia, 1936) and Fletcher M. Green, *Constitutional Development in the South Atlantic States, 1776–1860* (Chapel Hill, 1930), Chs. 1–3.*

* Available in paper back.

The Confederation, 1781–1787

The Articles of Confederation was the first constitution of the United States and experiences under it profoundly influenced the founding fathers. There is no modern general survey of the Confederation period but Andrew C. McLoughlin, *Confederation and Constitution* (New York, 1905) is useful. Merrill Jensen, *The Articles of Confederation* (Madison, 1940), is an important but controversial interpretation of the origins of the Articles from a Beardian perspective that was most cogently challenged by Oscar and Mary F. Handlin, "Radicals and Conservatives in Massachusetts," *New England Quarterly,* XVII (1944), 343–355. Merrill Jensen's *The New Nation* (1950) * is a major reinterpretation that makes a strong case for the viability of the Confederation without adequately explaining why contemporaries were less impressed with its virtues. One of the best ways to understand this period is through Richard P. McCormick's *Experiment in Independence, New Jersey in the Critical Period, 1781–1789* (New Brunswick, 1950). Also helpful is a review of the historiography by Richard B. Morris, "The Confederation Period and American History," *William and Mary Quarterly,* 3rd series, XIII (1956), 139–156.

The Federal Constitution

SOURCE MATERIALS

The basic documents for a study of the framing and ratification of the Federal Constitution are readily available. In addition to the various editions of *The Federalist Papers,** students can study the Philadelphia Convention through Max Farrand's, *Records of the Federal Convention of 1787* (4 vols., New Haven, 1911–1937).* The debates in the state ratifying conventions have been collected in Jonathan Elliot, *Debates in the Several State Conventions on the Adoption of the Federal Constitution* (5 vols., Philadelphia, 1861). And Cecilia Kenyon has conveniently collected and arranged the arguments of the opponents of the Constitution in *The Antifederalists* (Indianapolis, 1966) * with an introduction that analyzes the opposition's political thought.

* Available in paper back.

GENERAL SURVEYS

There are many narrative histories of the formation of the Constitution. Among the best are Carl Van Doren, *The Great Rehearsal* (New York, 1948), Charles Warren, *The Making of the Constitution* (Boston, 1928), and the most recent, Clinton Rossiter, *1787: The Grand Convention* (New York, 1966).

THE HISTORIOGRAPHICAL CONTROVERSY

Although the modern controversy stems mainly from Charles A. Beard's *An Economic Interpretation of the Constitution* (New York, 1911),* Beard was influenced by Orin G. Libby's *Geographical Distribution of the Vote of the Thirteen States on the Federal Constitution, 1787–1788* (Madison, 1894) * which was the first important attempt to explain the Constitution as the product of social conflict, in this case sectional rivalries.

Although Beard's book met a hostile reception when it appeared, it captured the hearts and minds of a generation of American historians caught up in the progressive view of the nation's past. Two early revisionist rumblings appeared in state studies: Philip A. Crowl, "Anti-Federalism in Maryland, 1787–1788," *William and Mary Quarterly*, 3rd series, IV, (1947), 446–469 and Robert Thomas, "The Virginia Convention of 1788: A Critique of Beard's *'An Economic Interpretation of the Constitution'*," *Journal of Southern History*, XIX (1953), 83–72. Richard Hofstadter explored the intellectual milieu of Beard's work in "Beard and the Constitution; The History of an Idea," *American Quarterly*, II (1950), 195–213. The two major full length attacks on Beard are Robert E. Brown, *Charles Beard and the Constitution, a Critical Analysis of 'An Economic Interpretation of the Constitution'* (Princeton, 1956),* which critically examines the internal consistency of Beard's argument and his use of data and Forrest McDonald, *We the People, the Economic Origins of the Constitution* (Chicago, 1958),* which retraces Beard's footsteps and attempts to refute him line by line. While rejecting Beard, Linda Grant de Pauw, *The Eleventh Pillar: New York State and the Federal Constitution* (New York, 1966) attempts to reconstruct what actually happened in the important state of New York.

The attack on Beard has resulted in attempts to find other patterns of explanation for the ratification conflict. The most interesting is Cecilia Kenyon's "Men of Little Faith: The Anti-Federalists on the

* Available in paper back.

Nature of Representative Government," *William and Mary Quarterly, Series,* XIII (1955), 3–43, which suggests the conflict was ideological in nature without explaining the sources of differences between the supporters and opponents of the Constitution. Stanley Elkins and Eric McKitrick, *The Founding Fathers, Young Men of the Revolution* (Washington, 1962) have sought the key in generational differences between the two groups, another thesis that founders on oversimplification. Another original, but highly idiosyncratic thesis is Forrest McDonald's, "The Anti-Federalists, 1781–1789," *Wisconsin Magazine of History,* XLVI (1963), 206–214.

Beard has not gone without defenders. Chief among them are Jackson T. Main, *The Antifederalists: Critics of the Constitution, 1781–1788* (Chapel Hill, 1961),* which advances a more complex version of the class conflict interpretation based on careful study of the states. Staughton Lynd has done likewise in smaller compass for New York in *Anti-Federalism in Dutchess County, New York* (Chicago, 1962). Lee Benson, *Turner and Beard: American Historical Writing Reconsidered* (Glencoe, 1960) * tries to restate Beard's interpretation to better account for the data.

POLITICAL THOUGHT

Some of the most interesting and illuminating studies have examined the political thought generated by the movement for the Federal Constitution. Gottfried Dietze's, *The Federalist* (Baltimore, 1960)* is an intensive reading of the *The Federalist Papers* by a student of political theory. Two articles by Douglass Adair are especially valuable: "The Tenth Federalist Revisited," *William and Mary Quarterly,* 3rd series, VIII (1951), 48–67 offers a fresh reading of the document that provided Beard with important evidence for an economic interpretation; " 'That Politics May be Reduced to a Science,' David Hume, James Madison and the Tenth Federalist," *Huntington Library Quarterly,* XX (1957), 343–360 traces the origins of Madison's innovative notions for reconstructing the republic as a federal system. Alpheus Mason, "The Federalist, A Split Personality," *American Historical Review,* LVII (1952), 625–643, argues that there were important differences between Hamilton's and Madison's contributions to the Federalist Papers. Benjamin Wright explores one of the principal assumptions underlying any political system in *"The Federalist* on the Nature of Political Man," *Ethics,* LIX (1949), no. 2, part 2. Finally, three biographical studies

* Available in paper back.

offer another useful approach to the founding fathers: Irving Brant, *James Madison: the Nationalist, 1780–1787* (Indianapolis, 1948) and *James Madison: Father of the Constitution, 1787–1800* (Indianapolis, 1950) ; Clinton Rossiter, *Alexander Hamilton and the American Constitution* (New York) ; 1964) ; John R. Howe, *The Changing Political Thought of John Adams* (Princeton, 1966) is the best study of the most important constitutional theorist of the revolutionary generation although Adams did not attend the Philadelphia Convention.